MW01644210

LEAD BY SERVING NEEDS

How Servant Leadership Empowers Managers to Meet 8 Essential Needs and Build Trust, Loyalty, and High Performance

DAVID SPUNGIN

With admiration and appreciation

To the United States Armed Forces, Firefighters, Law Enforcement, and Emergency Responders

Thank you for your service

TABLE OF CONTENTS

Introduction 1

PART I: THE CORE PRINCIPLES 9

1. Principle #1 Mission First, People Always 11
2. Principle #2 Character Defines Your Destiny 15
3. Principle #3 Leaders Eat Last 25
4. Principle #4 Be Redundant to Get Promoted 29
5. Principle #5 Leaders Leave a Legacy 33

PART II: SERVING THE PERSON 37

6. The Need to Be Seen 39
7. The Need to Be Heard 53

PART III: SERVING THE WORK 65

8. The Need for Autonomy 67
9. The Need to be Challenged 87
10. The Need for Recognition 103

PART IV: SERVING THE TEAM 117

11. The Need for Direction 119
12. The Need for Protection 139
13. The Need for Connection 155

PART V: CALL TO ACTION 167

14. Servant Leaders Wanted 169

About the Author 175

References 176

Endnotes 181

INTRODUCTION

My passion has always been leadership. As a kid, I gravitated toward leadership roles—whether striving to be the captain of my sports teams or running for class president. Leadership came naturally to me, and I enjoyed the responsibility. So, when West Point showed interest in me during high school, it felt like a perfect fit. Little did I know how much I had to learn about leading others! My journey at West Point was arduous, and I barely made it through the first two years. Yet, the experience deepened my passion and commitment. When it came time to choose a major, I selected Leadership Development. My peers teased me for pursuing this at an "engineering school," but it turned out to be one of the smartest decisions I ever made.

For the next ten years of my life, I had the honor of leading Cavalrymen in the U.S. Army. The theories I had studied came alive as I practiced leadership every day. What a gift it was to be twenty-three years old and tasked with leading a unit of seasoned soldiers. Yes, technically, I was "in charge," but I wasn't their leader until I earned it. Leadership wasn't granted with rank; it had to be proven through actions and example. I failed often, but each failure taught me invaluable lessons. Ultimately, I discovered that Servant Leadership is the most effective way to lead. Period.

Since then, I've spent most of my adult life facilitating leadership programs and coaching executives. I often reflect on how blessed I am to do what I love and wonder how I got this amazing gig. Yet, getting here was not blind luck; it was a mix of a little talent and a lot of hard work. Early in my career, I noticed many great leaders struggled with teaching others how to lead. They were natural leaders, but teaching others leadership was challenging. Conversely, many brilliant instructors I encountered were not experienced, real-world leaders. They could teach theory effectively but hadn't formally "walked the talk." This gap became my sweet spot. I've had the privilege of leading teams in both military and business settings, and I happen to have a knack for teaching leadership concepts in a relatable, actionable way.

The key to my success lies in sharing experiences without giving prescriptive advice. Instead, I create conditions that allow others to discover leadership for themselves. No one can make someone else a better leader; they can only provide guidance that produces choices. A person must then choose to lead, a decision that can only come from within. Understanding this principle has been instrumental in helping others unlock their full potential.

In walking this path, I've also learned a lot about myself. I have a strong bias for action, brevity, results, and pragmatism. In other words, I'm impatient! While this trait can hold me back at times, it's also a gift. When it comes to leadership books, I want practical answers. I'm not interested in abstract theories or long-winded anecdotes. I want to know what to do and how to do it. I prefer to put a book down and immediately apply what I've learned. This is where I got stuck with Servant Leadership.

Don't get me wrong, I deeply admire Servant Leadership, and Robert Greenleaf's philosophy has withstood the test of time[1]. Yet, most books on Servant Leadership today are still broadly principle-based, leaving readers to figure out the specific actions on their own. This book aims to change that.

Lead by Serving Needs will give you the tools and frameworks to help you translate philosophy into action. While my approach here is more prescriptive than usual, this is purposeful due to the reasons mentioned above. At the same time, I've included assessments, reflective questions, and deliberate practices to ensure you stay engaged in the process of self-discovery. These will help build self-awareness and give you options for immediately practicing Servant Leadership in your daily life.

That said, the first few chapters focus on principles. I realize this might seem contradictory, given my critique of theoretical approaches. But bear with me—there's a reason for this structure.

In short, values drive behavior. We can learn practical strategies for Servant Leadership, but without the right mindset, those strategies won't stick. Thinking like a Servant Leader is the foundation. Once your mindset aligns, your actions will naturally follow. This step is crucial because two major obstacles stand in our way: our genetics and our ego.

By nature, we are designed to be selfish. Evolutionary psychologists have written extensively about this. In his seminal book *The Selfish Gene*, Richard Dawkins explained how our genes prioritize our survival and that there is no gene for altruistic or selfless behavior. According to his research, even acts of care for others often serve an underlying self-interest[2]. While that may paint our human essence in a bad light, it's important to acknowledge where we start, and it's not insurmountable.

Think of yourself as a computer running selfish software. You may be programmed this way, but you can upgrade your system. Humans have the unique ability to exercise free will, reprogram innate tendencies, and choose selfless actions. This is the essence of becoming a Servant Leader.

It is not just our genes that stand in our way to becoming servant leaders; the ego is an equally formidable obstacle. Leaders often get promoted due to their competence. They've proven they can deliver results, and the organization hopes to multiply those results through greater responsibility. Promotion usually means title, position, power, and authority. Not to mention the additional salary, perks, and privileges that come with the territory. The ego eats all this up, and the more it eats, the bigger it grows. Advancement becomes "proof" of how smart and capable we are. This elevated sense of self-importance makes it harder to stay grounded. Ego-driven leaders can lose sight of their values and fall into self-serving behaviors.

So, what mindsets should Servant Leaders adopt? Let's start by identifying the wrong way to think:

- This place would fall apart without me. (I'm the key to our success)
- I'll focus my attention on those who can benefit me. (My time is too valuable for those who can't help me)

- Success requires me to be more successful than others. (Advancement requires win-lose scenarios)
- Leaders don't make mistakes. (I need to look good at all times)
- Leaders are smarter than others. (I need to be the smartest person in the room)
- My team is below me in the hierarchy. (They should respect my authority)

You might think, "That's not me at all!" Yet, these tendencies can show up subtly and situationally. Selfish environments can bring out the worst in us, and we can never underestimate their power to shape our behavior. One famous example of this occurred in 2001 when Enron Corporation collapsed in spectacular fashion as its fraudulent accounting practices were exposed. The executive leaders at Enron were likely not bad people, but cultural pressures encouraged greed and selfishness to transpire. As the scandal unraveled, 25,000 people lost their jobs, and their pension plans were completely wiped out.

A more recent example occurred in 2016 when Theranos, led by Elizabeth Holmes, misled investors, regulators, and the public with false claims concerning the efficacy of their blood testing technology. Holmes was a brilliant and successful leader, but her ego steered her to create a culture of deception and intimidation when the data didn't align with her plan. The result was the demise of the once-promising company and a staggering $600 million in losses to investors.

The first step in overcoming these self-serving mindsets is noticing when they show up for you. For example, ask yourself, "In what situations do I feel compelled to prove my intelligence/value?" Or "When do I put my team's needs on hold because I have important work to do?" Building self-awareness of when these mindsets show up only comes through deliberate reflection.

Now, let's look at some mindsets that foster Servant Leadership.

- How can I make myself replaceable? (this makes me more valuable and promotable)
- Who needs my attention the most? (attention is currency to be invested in others)
- How can I make my team members more successful? (when they succeed, I succeed)
- Leaders are human and make mistakes. (take risks, fail fast, fail forward)

- Leaders surround themselves with smarter people. (it makes my job easier)
- I work for my team, not the other way around. (my title exists, so I have the power to serve)

As you read these, notice your reaction. Did any feel uncomfortable? That discomfort is likely your ego pushing back. It's normal. Recognizing this resistance is part of the process.

When I read these, my ego says things like…

- What do you mean by replaceable? I'd much rather feel valuable.
- Constantly giving people my attention is exhausting.
- Mistakes? I'd rather not! That's how leaders fail!
- Being smart is a good thing. People respect you more when you demonstrate intelligence.
- I've worked hard for others to achieve my position, and others should have to do the same for me. Those are the rules of the game.

Maybe some similar thoughts emerged for you? You have to flip the script if you want to become a Servant Leader! Unfortunately, this is more easily said than done. Since most self-serving behavior happens unconsciously, humans must adopt conscious intervention strategies. To help reinforce the right mindsets, memorable sayings or acronyms can be useful. For example:

- Fake it until you make it (confidence is a self-fulling prophecy)
- Be the change you wish to see in the world (stop complaining and lead by example)
- YOLO–You only live once (live boldly and take more risks)
- When life gives you lemons, make lemonade (remain optimistic when facing adversity)
- Sometimes you win, and sometimes you learn (there are no losses, only valuable lessons)
- You catch more flies with honey than with vinegar (don't confront, instead persuade)
- WWJD—What would Jesus do? (consider your actions and their impact on others)

If you believe in the principles behind the sayings, then they can help your brain access the right thinking at the right times. In this way, I've developed five Core Principles to anchor this book:

1. Mission First, People Always
2. Character Defines Your Destiny
3. Leaders Eat Last
4. Be Redundant to Get Promoted
5. Leaders Leave a Legacy

These principles act as the foundation for everything we'll cover. Remember that the path to effective Servant Leadership is one of being before doing. If you study, internalize, and embody these principles, the doing part will unfold naturally.

The remainder of the book focuses on the specific needs a leader should focus on serving to be successful. While the eight needs identified are not all-encompassing, they are what I consider to be the most important. Taking a needs-based approach makes Servant Leadership more practical and actionable. It's a simple concept. Identify and assess the needs of your team, then take action to ensure they are taken care of. Do so consistently, and your team will bend over backward to make you successful. The eight critical needs are to be seen and heard, to operate autonomously, to be challenged and recognized, and to have direction, protection, and connection.

I've created an infographic summarizing the book's core concepts. You can download a color copy of this and additional supporting resources at www.davidspungin.com.

Download Your Free Additional Resources

LEAD BY SERVING NEEDS

How Servant Leadership Empowers Managers to
Meet 8 Essential Needs and Build Trust, Loyalty, and High Performance

Core Principles

1. Mission First, People Always
2. Character Defines Your Destiny
3. Leaders Eat Last
4. Be Redundant to Get Promoted
5. Leaders Leave a Legacy

The Person

Need to be Seen
Enhance approachability and invest your attention.

Need to be Heard
Unplug, get present, and listen for emotions.

The Work

Need for Autonomy
Empower people by delegating, providing intent, and coaching to outcomes.

Need for Challenge
Set high expectations, provide feedback, and maintain accountability.

Need for Recognition
Praise graciously and often. Look for the good and make others the hero.

The Team

Need for Direction
Cast a vision, create understanding, provide clarity, and be agile to beat VUCA.

Need for Protection
Shield the team from politics, dysfunction, and distractions. Keep focused on real priorities.

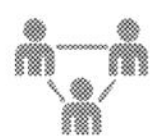

Need for Connection
Create space for the team to build cohesion and a shared identity.

I hope that this book makes Servant Leadership more accessible to more people. When leaders genuinely serve, they create a better world. They foster happier and more engaged workplaces. They build environments where people fulfill their potential and take pride in their team. Yet, perhaps more importantly, the impact extends well beyond the workplace. Happy, engaged, and fulfilled employees are more present and available for family and friends when they get off work. In this way, Servant Leaders indirectly strengthen communities and society. Now, that's a purpose worth striving for. Let's create a world of Servant Leaders together!

THE CORE PRINCIPLES

1

PRINCIPLE #1
MISSION FIRST, PEOPLE ALWAYS

In the high-stakes world of aerospace engineering, Sven led a team tasked with designing a critical component for a next-generation satellite. The deadline was nonnegotiable, and the pressure was immense. As the weeks wore on, the stress began to take a toll on his team. Morale was slipping, and late nights were becoming the norm. His team began to bicker with one another over trivial things. Sven knew pushing his engineers harder would get the project done, but at what cost?

If you were in Sven's shoes, what would you do? Would you press on to meet the deadline or risk missing it to care for your team? It's a challenging question to answer. On the one hand, leaders exist to deliver results. Leaders who fail to get results usually don't remain leaders for long! They get fired, marginalized, or replaced. Leadership roles can be fleeting because leaders are judged by their most recent outcomes. Therefore, leaders must always prioritize mission accomplishment and do what it takes to get the job done.

Yet, leaders rarely achieve anything on their own. Success comes through the efforts of others, making it essential to care for your people. If your team is disengaged, unmotivated, or dysfunctional, who will accomplish the mission?

They need your presence, guidance, and inspiration. Ironically, when leaders focus on caring for their people, mission accomplishment often takes care of itself.

The phrase "Mission First, People Always" is most often attributed to the U.S. military, particularly the Army and Marine Corps, where it's deeply ingrained in their culture. I first encountered this saying in the army and found it equally helpful later in corporate environments. Yes, it's a bit cliché, but it's also a sound reminder of where leaders should focus their attention. Leaders today are bombarded with distractions. It's easy for their time and energy to be stolen. However, if a leader's efforts are centered on mission accomplishment and caring for their people, they will likely succeed.

Mission-Focused vs. People-Focused Leaders

Mission Focus	People Focus
Emphasis on work facilitation	Emphasis on interaction facilitation
Focus on structure, roles and tasks	Focus on relationships, well-being, and motivation
Producing results is the priority	Care for team members is the priority
Emphasis on goals setting and achievement	Emphasis on communication and team health

So, to answer our original question of what is more important, it's not "either/or," it's "yes/and." We need to focus on both mission accomplishment and care for our people. However, in my experience coaching leaders, I've noticed that most people are predisposed to excel at one over the other.

This is primarily a function of one's innate personality preferences. You either have a preference for tasks or people. Task-oriented leaders thrive on setting goals, structuring solutions, and driving execution. People-oriented leaders excel at reading group dynamics, motivating teams, and building winning cultures. What is your preference? If you had to prioritize one, which would it be?

You might wonder if either approach is more beneficial to a leader. In 2009, James Zenger studied the traits that make a boss a "great leader." The survey included 60,000 people and examined characteristics like results focus and social skills. Results focus was noted as having strong analytical skills with an intense motivation to move forward. Social skills were defined as combining attributes like communication and empathy. The findings were fascinating[3]:

- If a leader was **very strongly results-focused**, the chance of **being seen as a great leader was only 14%.**
- If a leader was **strong in social skills**, they were **seen as a great leader even less, at 12%.**
- However, for leaders who were **strong in both results focus and social skills**, the likelihood of **being seen as a great leader rose steeply to 72%**.

Clearly, having both traits is far better than having only one. Yet, fewer than 1% of leaders rate highly in both results orientation and social skills.[4] Complicating matters further, Andrew Lieberman's book *Social: Why Our Brains Are Wired to Connect* highlights the difficulty of excelling in both areas simultaneously.

He explains, "Our brains have made it difficult to be both socially and analytically focused at the same time. Even though thinking socially and analytically doesn't feel radically different, evolution built our brains with different networks for handling these two ways of thinking. These two networks function like a *neural seesaw*. In countless neuroimaging studies, the more one of these networks got more active, the more the other one got quieter. Although there are some exceptions, in general, engaging in one of the kinds of thinking makes it harder to engage in the other kind."

This is why it's crucial to understand your preference for mission accomplishment or caring for people. Effective Servant Leaders must excel in both areas, yet we are all wired to favor one. By becoming aware of your tendency, you can periodically pause and reflect on whether the situation requires shifting your focus. You don't need to be the rare 1% leader who excels at both simultaneously. Instead, know your people, read the situation, and focus fully on what's needed most at the moment.

Returning to Sven's predicament: if you naturally prefer a mission-first approach, you might press on and risk your team's well-being. You might rationalize it by thinking, "Missing the deadline could jeopardize the entire contract. What good is taking a break if we all lose our jobs?" However, this perspective ignores other risks. What if the deadline is met, but the quality suffers due to burnout, requiring costly rework? What if key team members quit because they feel overworked and undervalued? Or worse, what if a team member gets hurt driving home one night after working late and falling asleep at the wheel?

This is a moment when a mission-first leader should adapt to the situation. You could pause work for a day and organize a team lunch, followed by an open discussion about the challenges you all are facing. Then, encourage the team to share frustrations and suggestions. Not only does this provide space to vent, but it might also uncover solutions. The team might agree to leave early today, rest, and return fresh tomorrow, potentially regaining productivity and catching up.

Your people will never forget how you handle situations like these. If you focus only on the mission, people will notice your lack of care, and you will lose credibility and respect. Conversely, if you prioritize their well-being, they'll notice that too, inspiring loyalty and trust. Servant Leaders excel by maintaining a mission-first mindset while keeping an eye on their people and shifting focus when necessary.

2

PRINCIPLE #2
CHARACTER DEFINES YOUR DESTINY

During my time as a cadet, West Point's official purpose statement was, "To provide the nation with leaders of character who serve the common defense." While the wording has changed slightly since then, the emphasis on producing leaders of character remains steadfast.[5] But why such an emphasis on character? Why not prioritize developing leaders who simply win battles or wars? Isn't that what's most needed from Army officers? Or, why not produce visionary leaders who advance society in remarkable ways? While West Point graduates have historically contributed in such capacities—from walking on the moon to leading Fortune 500 companies—the academy's central emphasis remains on character. This focus is deliberate because character defines your destiny as a leader.

So, what does it mean to be a "leader of character"? And what must we practice to develop the character needed to become a Servant Leader? The good news is that the foundational values of Servant Leadership were likely introduced to you at an early age. Think about it: your average two-year-old embodies the mindset of a selfish leader. It's all about "me, me, me." Leadership expert James C. Hunter often jokes, "What's the difference between a really bad boss and a petulant child? The kid will grow up someday!" Bad bosses remain stuck in this selfish stage.

The road to character development begins early, perhaps as early as kindergarten. That's when we learn about kindness, sharing, including others, apologizing for mistakes, and taking responsibility for our actions. It's when we begin to transition from a me-centered world to one of shared responsibility.

Later in life, experiences like playing team sports, joining clubs like Boy Scouts or Girl Scouts, or attending church can further socialize us and strengthen our moral foundation. Yet, much of our character is shaped through life's trials and errors. We are what we repeatedly do, and our character is formed through what we practice most frequently. The problem is that we don't realize we are always practicing! We make hundreds of character choices every day.

Imagine this: tomorrow morning, you wake up with an ache somewhere in your body. Irritated, you face a choice—remain grumpy or push through your day with resilience and optimism. Later, someone cuts you off in traffic during your commute to work. You can angrily honk or remain calm and patient. Once at work, you open an email from a peer criticizing your team's performance. You can react defensively or choose accountability, empathy, and collaboration to address the issue.

It's not even 9 a.m., and already, the quality of your character is influencing your leadership effectiveness! These challenges could easily upset the best of us, and leaders are not expected to be perfect human beings. Yet, leaders are always on stage, and their daily choices reverberate through their teams, making disciplined self-management of emotions critical.

The Ladder of Inference

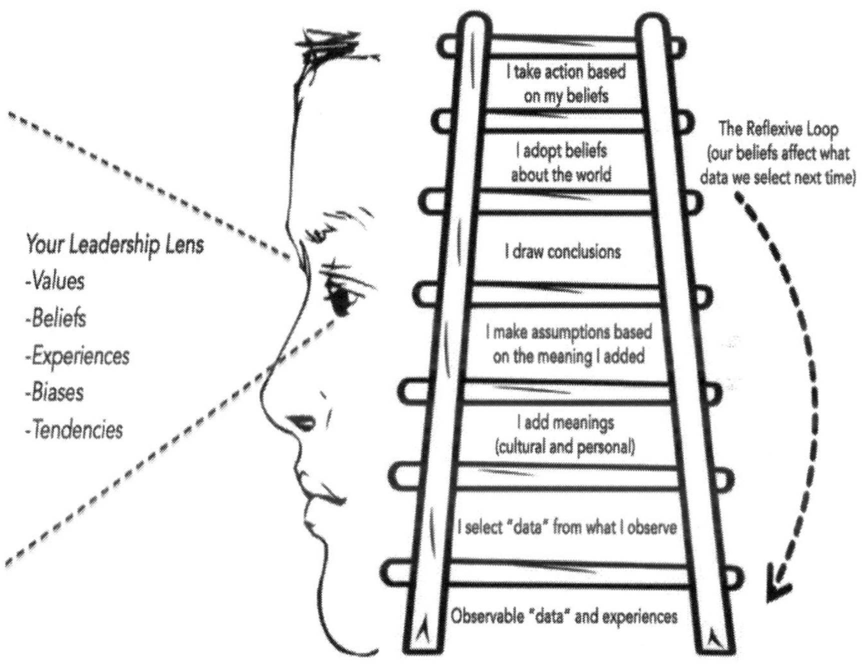

One of the best models for understanding how character impacts behavior is the Ladder of Inference, developed by Chris Argyris. Humans process an astounding 1.25 billion pieces of data per second. To avoid being overwhelmed, our brains rely on a "lens" to filter information and focus on what matters. This lens—comprising our values, beliefs, biases, and mindsets—adds meaning to our observations. That meaning includes assumptions, which inform our conclusions and drive our actions. Over time, our repeated actions reinforce or reshape our lens, solidifying our character.

Unfortunately, our lens is shaped by past experiences that we cannot change. Most of you reading this have already lived those formative years in your lives that determine the quality of your character today. However, regardless of our starting point, we all have the power to exercise free will daily. The key is becoming aware of how our current values, beliefs, and mindsets influence our choices. I often tell my coaching clients, "We are what we practice, and we are always practicing something!" Servant leaders train themselves to "observe their observer" to increase awareness of how their lens influences their choices, behavior, and character. With this awareness, we can make decisions more aligned with the character required for Servant Leadership.

While many qualities make up a Servant Leader's character, I believe these are most important: integrity, reliability, accountability, care, grit, and self-discipline. Additionally, these qualities are most effective when driven by an outward focus on others rather than self-interest. I appreciate how math equations can elegantly simplify complexity, so I've created this formula to help visualize my thinking.

$$\text{Leader's Character} = \frac{\underset{\text{Integrity}}{I} + \underset{\text{Reliable}}{R} + \underset{\text{Accountable}}{A} + \underset{\text{Caring}}{C} + \underset{\text{Grit}}{G} + \underset{\text{Disciplined}}{D}}{\underset{\text{Self-Orientation}}{S}}$$

Integrity is the foundation. The definition of integrity is twofold. First, it means being honest, moral, and principled. Second, it means the state of being whole and undivided. To have integrity means that your actions match your words (or thinking). There is no division between the two. If you are not a person of your word, bend the truth, or change your story based on your audience, people will have a hard time trusting you, and no one willingly follows someone they don't trust.

Integrity is not fixed; it's a daily practice. Leaders must work hard to demonstrate high integrity and protect it diligently. You are either moving towards or away from maintaining high integrity every day. A common pitfall is overcommitting. Leaders want to help and struggle to say no. So, they jam their calendars full of personal and professional commitments. Inevitably, they drop the ball. They come home late from work and miss dinner again. Or, they can't make it to their kid's basketball game they promised to attend. Work commitments often trump personal ones, but failing to honor personal commitments often leads to professional lapses later. Leaders do their best to always protect their word and close their "say-do gap." Don't "say it" if you can't "do it." If you said it and now realize you can't do it, renegotiate, but ensure you always follow through eventually.

Reliability means consistency. Do you show up the same way every day, regardless of stress? Are your decisions sound and predictable? Are you a loyal person? These are a few questions that followers unconsciously ask themselves. A leader's actions need to answer the mail with a resounding YES! It's about creating stability and predictability. Research shows that employees would prefer to work for a "screamer" boss who consistently and predictably loses their cool than a "Jekyll and Hyde" boss whom you can never tell how they might react to a situation.[6] Why? Inconsistent behavior breeds anxiety and mistrust. People can develop coping mechanisms for the screamer; we tune out, get thick-skinned, or avoid them. Yet, there is little we can do about inconsistent behavior. Sometimes, even the level of inconsistency is inconsistent! It's maddening and creates feelings of helplessness.

A common mistake leaders make is that they need to be more reliable in giving feedback to their team members. They can alternate between excessive praise one day and then nitpick them with demoralizing negative feedback the next. Or they give employees a "feedback sandwich," starting with positive feedback before switching to constructive feedback and finishing with positive feedback, all in the same conversation. All feedback is a gift, but these approaches to offering feedback often create confusion. "Am I doing well, or am I not doing well?" is the outcome. Anxiety breeds mistrust, and, once again, people don't follow leaders they don't trust.

Accountability is owning your responsibilities. Do you take pride in your work? Do you own your mistakes as much as your successes? Do you return the shopping cart or leave it in the parking lot? Okay, that last question may seem trivial, but the Shopping Cart Theory meme went viral as the ultimate litmus test of one's character, so clearly, it resonates with many people![7] Of all the leadership characteristics, accountability is perhaps the most difficult to learn. And let's be clear: it must be learned. I've yet to meet a human born without a strong predisposition to offer excuses, place blame, or get defensive when someone points out they messed up. West Point understands this well, and one of the first things a New Cadet learns is "The Four Responses." When an upperclassman asks you a question, you may only respond with 1) Yes Sir/Ma'am, 2) No Sir/Ma'am), or 3) NO EXCUSE SIR/MA'AM), or 4) Sir/Ma'am I do not understand. I capitalized the third response because usually, the louder you own it, the less trouble you will get in.

At first, it's exasperating. West Point recruits smart kids who like to have answers for everything. You want to say, "There's a perfectly good explanation for why I didn't do what was expected. You see, no one explained that to me. Also, New Cadet Csoka needed some help, so I got distracted with helping him." Instead, you must override your brain; the only answer you can provide is NO EXCUSE SIR/MA'AM! It almost feels like you are lying. You absolutely have an excuse, but leadership demands more. Over time, you learn that the unfortunate first rule of leadership is that everything is your fault. That's because while you might not be responsible for a mistake, you are always accountable for everything you and your team do. The sooner you can come to grips with this, the more prepared you will be to lead others.

Caring reflects your demeanor and approach to relationships. Do you prioritize others' needs, demonstrate empathy, and show compassion? The saying goes that people don't care about how much you know until they know how much you care. In leadership, competence is simply the price of admission. You must know your job to earn credibility and respect, but care is what earns people's trust. If people don't feel you genuinely care for them, they will be skeptical of your intentions. If you can't feel their pain points and show compassion, they will feel disconnected from you and see you as unapproachable.

This is why empathy is the king of all leadership behaviors. When we do empathy well, we cannot fail but build high trust with others. This was a leadership lesson I learned later in life. While West Point did a great job at teaching personal accountability, let's say that empathy wasn't its highest priority. My subsequent years in the Army didn't do wonders for my empathy development either. It wasn't until I had a family and spent time in corporate America that I started to see the power of empathy in action. Perhaps you are already a highly empathetic and caring person. If so, well done, and keep it up! However, if these skills are something you could still work on, I highly encourage you to practice more empathy in your life. Nothing will improve the quality of your relationships faster and more substantively.

Grit is your ability to persevere, be determined, show resilience, and have a strong work ethic, especially in the face of challenges, setbacks, and obstacles. It's the ability to stay committed to long-term goals, even when the journey is grueling. Gritty individuals are known for their passion, dedication, and willingness to put in sustained effort over time. Grit also requires patience as it involves delayed gratification. Gritty people often have to "embrace the suck" and won't see any rewards for their efforts for some time.

The concept of grit gained prominence through the work of psychologist Angela Duckworth, who, not so ironically, conducted much of her research at West Point. She set out to try to understand why some cadets quit and why some cadets persevered through the grueling four years and graduated. Specifically, she sought to understand if specific characteristics lent someone to be more successful. Duckworth's team studied 11,258 cadets as they entered the academy over a decade, and her findings concluded that "while strength and brain power all contributed to helping the 81 percent of West Point cadets who ultimately graduated from the school, the study found that "grit" proved to be the most significant factor."[8]

This is all too familiar for me, as I came close to quitting West Point several times during my first two years there. At one point, I enrolled at Virginia Tech, had a roommate lined up, and was days away from leaving forever. As a young man, I hadn't failed much before. Yet, West Point has a way of ensuring that everyone fails at something, and I wasn't coping very well. I struggled in chemistry and physics and had to attend summer school for both classes. This meant I lost out on the precious few weeks of summer vacation that most Cadets enjoyed. Failing classes and being unable to go home greatly affected me. I was isolated, overwhelmed, and feeling inadequate. It was one of the darkest periods in my life.

I wanted to cut and run, but the oddest thing kept me around. When cadets quit, they typically hand over all their uniform items to their friends so they have extras. This is an excellent deal for the recipients as extra uniforms meant doing less laundry. The key to this story is that every Cadet clothing item has to be labeled with their last name and the last four digits of their social security number: every jacket, every pair of pants, even your underwear. So, over the years, I'd collected many items from my friends who had called it quits. I remember sitting in my room just days from packing myself up and looking at a physical training shirt with SMITH 2456 labeled in marker on the back of the collar. I thought to myself, "Someone will inherit my shirt if I leave. They will see my name and say, too bad Spungin didn't make it." It lit a fire in me! Call it pride, ego, or whatever you'd like. It was just what I needed to find my resolve and develop more grit!

Discipline can mean a lot of things. Demonstrating self-discipline can mean your ability to avoid temptation, manage your time and stress, or even uphold your physical appearance. Yes, these are all essential aspects of being self-disciplined. However, the most important kind of self-discipline is maintaining composure and managing difficult emotions. Emotional self-discipline is imperative for a leader. This is because leaders' emotions are contagious, and their authority magnifies their impact.

When a leader smiles regularly and exhibits a positive, optimistic attitude, people tend to feel good and carry that positivity with them throughout their day. This can have a ripple effect and can flow from person to person through a team. Unfortunately, the same ripple effect can occur when a leader exudes negativity. Sure, leaders have bad days, too, but the best leaders can exercise self-discipline and not allow their moods and emotions to take over.

Emotional self-discipline is a distinct aspect of our character that's honed over time. While some personality types are more emotional than others, none of us start perfectly at this. How well can you notice what you are feeling (in the moment), understand how that's impacting you, and choose to think or act in a way best suited for more successful outcomes? A leader who remains calm, cool, and collected under stress inspires confidence in their followers. When facing audacious objectives and obstacles, a leader transforms anxiety into excitement and confidently moves forward. When feeling embarrassed because they've been criticized publicly, a leader finds the strength to exhibit humility and curiosity rather than retaliate. Leaders exhibiting emotional self-discipline earn our respect and admiration because we all recognize how difficult this is.

Finally, **self-orientation** determines the emphasis you place on yourself versus others. If you review all the previously noted components of character, effectiveness in each is determined by our ability to override our selfish instincts. For example, one might be dishonest about a mistake to avoid facing the consequences. While they've saved themselves from the pain of discomfort, they've lowered their integrity and accountability. Or someone might give up on a project because it's easier to quit and they are tired. They may be reducing their stress level, but it's at the expense of developing grit, and their reliability might also take a hit.

I could go on with examples for each characteristic; it always comes down to choosing the harder right over the easier desire to serve oneself. This is what makes Servant Leadership so powerful! Servant Leaders do what others often cannot. They override instincts, choose sacrifice, and act for the greater good. Developing the character needed to serve often requires personal sacrifice, but the rewards—trust, respect, and meaningful impact—are immeasurable. While the road is less traveled, the destination is worth the effort.

3

PRINCIPLE #3
LEADERS EAT LAST

Imagine for a moment that you are a young Lieutenant in the U.S. Army. You are in charge of about forty soldiers, including several Non-Commissioned Officers (NCOs) who are older and more experienced than you. A big part of your job involves conducting field exercises to train in warfighting tasks as a team. These exercises typically take place in remote training areas and can last anywhere from a few days to months.

Depending on where you're stationed, the weather is often one of the biggest challenges. From the frigid cold of Alaska to the blistering heat of Texas, the environment can make these exercises downright miserable. We had a saying: "If it ain't raining, then we ain't training!" The idea was that "real" training happens under the toughest conditions. For this story, let's say you and your platoon are out in the field, cold, wet, and rain-soaked. HOOAH![9]

Now, try to recall how it feels after days of poor sleep. You're lucky to get two to four hours a night during field exercises. You and your soldiers are utterly exhausted as you prepare for tonight's mission. Your hands are freezing as you scribble out your orders. Looking around, you see your soldiers huddled under makeshift rain shelters, shivering and covered in mud. Suddenly, morale gets a huge boost. The First Sergeant arrives with the chow truck! Nothing raises spirits faster than hot food in a moment like this. You realize how hungry you are. As the ranking officer, you have the authority to jump the line and eat first. After all, you have important plans to finalize, so it makes sense to eat your meal quickly and get back to work.

But you don't jump the line. Instead of grabbing a plate, you pick up the serving spoon. One by one, you serve your soldiers as they line up for food. You serve yourself only after everyone, including the lowest-ranking private, has eaten their fill. By the time you eat, the food is cold, and there's not much left—but that doesn't matter. What matters is that you've shown your team you prioritize their needs over your own. This small act of service speaks volumes about your values and who you are as a leader. It demonstrates empathy, self-awareness, and discipline. More importantly, it's an investment in the future. When your team knows you'll always put them first, they'll go to great lengths to ensure your success.

Now, imagine the alternative. What if you ate first? Some might understand your reasoning—your responsibilities and tight deadlines. However, most of your unit would see something different. They'd see a leader using their rank to get hot food before them. Worse, what if the last soldier in line didn't get any food because it ran out? You'd be sitting there with a full stomach, feeling guilty, and the soldier's trust in you would plummet. Would they willingly follow you into battle one day? Probably not. Their motivation would wane, and your credibility would take a serious hit. This is why "Leaders Eat Last" is a cornerstone of Servant Leadership. Putting others first earns their respect and loyalty.

Modern workplaces usually don't have chow trucks, so how does "Leaders Eat Last" apply to you? This principle manifests in many ways in professional environments, often in ways leaders may not realize. One of the most visible examples is company perks and privileges. Leaders frequently have access to things that others do not. They get the preferred corner office. They receive a primo parking spot right up front. They fly business class or use the company jet. I've even seen some leaders with private elevators and bathrooms at work. While these perks are designed to reward hard work and confirm status, they often create unapproachable and disconnected leaders.

Servant Leaders understand they are always being observed and carefully consider how their actions are perceived. Instead of taking the corner office, they give it to the top salesperson. They convert the best parking spot into "Employee of the Month" parking. They travel the same way their team does and take the same elevator, using the opportunity to chat with employees. These small gestures of humility and service go a long way in building trust and connection. Unfortunately, many leaders fail here, rationalizing their behavior with thoughts like, "I've earned these privileges," or "No one will notice if I use them." But people do notice, and over time, this erodes credibility. Servant Leaders recognize the value of setting aside their ego because the long-term trust and loyalty they earn far outweigh any short-term perks.

There are also subtler ways leaders can unintentionally violate the "Leaders Eat Last" principle. Consider where you sit during team meetings. Many leaders automatically take the head of the table, but mixing up seating arrangements can foster connection and show a willingness to share power. Similarly, when brainstorming ideas, who speaks first and who speaks last? Leaders often dominate the discussion early on, steering the conversation in the "right" direction. A Servant Leader will instead pose a question and facilitate dialogue, hearing from everyone before entering the conversation. These small but meaningful actions demonstrate self-awareness and an inclusive mindset, building trust within the team.

The next time your position offers you an advantage, ask yourself, "Am I eating before my team does?" Picture those cold, hungry soldiers standing in the rain. Choose to put others first. Not only will you gain their respect and loyalty, but you'll also feel deeply rewarded. While perks and privileges may feel satisfying in the moment, the fulfillment of serving others is far greater.

4

PRINCIPLE #4
BE REDUNDANT TO GET PROMOTED

Pranav was a leader I coached at a software development company. When we began working together, he managed a team of twenty and was highly respected in his role. Under Pranav's strong leadership, his team consistently exceeded its goals. But it wasn't just Pranav's team—the entire company was thriving, experiencing rapid growth and a hiring boom. Pranav's responsibilities expanded along with his team, and he felt proud of what he'd accomplished, both personally and professionally.

One day, during a coaching session, I noticed a change in his tone. Usually upbeat and enthusiastic, he sounded deflated. Concerned, I asked if something was wrong. He sighed before admitting, "David, I don't get it. I'm delivering on all my objectives. I'm being told I'm a high-potential leader. But I just got passed over for a promotion."

His peer, someone on a similar career trajectory, had been promoted to Senior Director, a role Pranav had also been eligible for. When I asked why he thought he was overlooked, he replied, "I don't know. They said I'm too valuable in my current role. Can you believe that load of crap? That's just something they say to make you feel better about being passed over."

I responded, "What if that's the truth? But not in the way you think. Being irreplaceable in your current role might actually be holding you back."

His expression shifted from confusion to realization. It clicked: Pranav was the linchpin of his team's success. Moving him out of that role wasn't in the company's best interest. It was time for him to redefine success. He needed to make himself redundant.

You might be thinking, "What are you talking about? Being redundant is a bad thing!" After all, people are often laid off due to redundancies. If two people can both do the same job, someone usually has to go. Yes, there may be some truth to that. But for Servant Leaders, being redundant isn't about job security—it's about scaling their impact. To reach more people and take on bigger challenges, they need to be promotable. And the fastest way to get promoted is to build a team of leaders who can thrive in your absence.

This mindset can be a difficult shift for some. Many leaders define their value by being the go-to problem solver, the subject matter expert, or the firefighter. They take pride in delivering results and accumulate so much institutional knowledge that they become indispensable in their role. However, this focus on execution often comes at the expense of developing others.

Servant Leaders understand the importance of growing their people. They understand their people's motivations and aspirations. They invest time in learning what motivates their team members, understanding their strengths and skill gaps, and identifying their learning styles. They consistently match tasks with growth opportunities and actively coach, mentor, and train. Some leaders, fearing a loss of relevance, hold back certain knowledge to maintain their value. This is a mistake that stifles the team's growth. Servant Leaders, on the other hand, strive to avoid being bottlenecks. They empower their people to take on challenges independently, creating bandwidth for themselves to focus on higher-level priorities.

When senior leadership sees a Servant Leader's team operating effectively without constant oversight, they recognize that leader's ability to scale their impact. They trust the leader's judgment and feel confident placing them in roles where their influence can extend across the organization. In this way, making yourself redundant becomes a hallmark of effective leadership and sets the stage for promotion.

Every day presents opportunities to create learning moments for your team. Help them see perspectives they might otherwise miss. Encourage them to think bigger, push their limits, and support them as they stretch. As part of this knowledge transfer, I share specific skills and techniques for developing others in Chapter 8 ("The Need for Autonomy") and Chapter 9 ("The Need for Challenge"). These chapters detail how Servant Leaders use feedback and coaching to accelerate growth and build strong, independent teams.

5

PRINCIPLE #5
LEADERS LEAVE A LEGACY

Sports enthusiasts love debating GOAT (Greatest of All Time) lists, and reading people's opinions is always fun. Many enjoy arguing about the GOAT of basketball: LeBron James or Michael Jordan? Tom Brady is often crowned the GOAT of the NFL, Lionel Messi holds the title in soccer, and Serena Williams is widely regarded as the GOAT of women's tennis. These discussions tend to focus on athletes, but one of my favorite GOAT lists ranks NFL head coaches.

When deciding on the GOAT of NFL coaches, you need clear criteria to evaluate candidates. You could look at win-loss percentages, playoff appearances, Super Bowl wins, or seasons making the playoffs. However, one list I came across went beyond these baseline stats. This list argued that the true measure of coaching greatness is how many assistant coaches under their mentorship go on to become head coaches. In other words, greatness is measured by having a "Tree"—a legacy of developing others. Legendary coaches like Vince Lombardi, George Halas, and Hank Stram didn't make this particular list because their protégés didn't achieve significant success.[10]

But take a look at Bill Walsh's coaching tree, and you'll quickly see why he stands out.

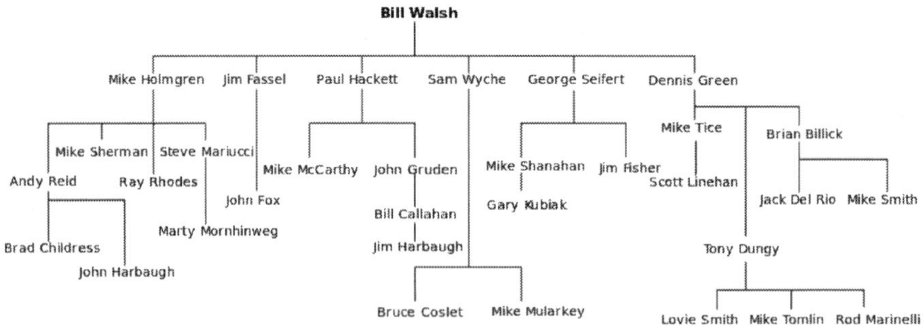

Bill Walsh wasn't just a three-time Super Bowl champion (XVI, XIX, XXIII) or the NFL Coach of the Year in 1981. He was also a phenomenal mentor. He developed coaches like Mike Holmgren, Paul Hackett, George Seifert, Dennis Green, and Jim Fassel. These individuals alone have six Super Bowl appearances and three Lombardi trophies among them. Then there are others, like Jon Gruden, Mike Shanahan, Brian Billick, Jeff Fisher, Mike McCarthy, Steve Mariucci, Gary Kubiak, Andy Reid, and the Harbaugh brothers. Together, they add thirteen Super Bowl appearances, nine championship rings, and countless playoff wins to the legacy Walsh created. Talk about leaving a lasting impact!

While Walsh was a master strategist on the football field, his true gift lay in mentoring and developing his staff. Returning to *Principle #4—Be Redundant to Get Promoted*—Walsh clearly prioritized the development of those around him. His commitment to transferring knowledge and pushing his team to their full potential created a ripple effect of success. Former COO of Facebook Sheryl Sandberg put it well: "Leadership is about making others better as a result of your presence and making sure that impact lasts in your absence." Walsh's influence on the game of football endures because of the leaders he nurtured along the way.

Servant Leaders understand the importance of playing the long game. They define success by the impact they have on others and their communities. Every day presents opportunities to invest in the future, and they seize those moments to help others grow personally and professionally. They know that strong communities—built on collaboration, teamwork, and relationships—are the foundation of a thriving society. For Servant Leaders, the focus is always on others and the collective good.

Servant Leaders also know that a leader's true impact isn't measured while they're holding the torch; it's revealed when the torch is passed. Legacy matters to them. This perspective makes them less influenced by short-term pressures and more willing to make tough decisions for long-term benefits. They can accept quarterly losses if they mean consistent growth in the future. They remain committed to strategic goals rather than reacting impulsively to market shifts. This mindset might sometimes make them unpopular, but Servant Leaders understand that leadership isn't a popularity contest. They're focused on how they will be remembered and the outcomes they leave behind.

On that note, how a leader is remembered is a funny thing. Often, we judge leaders by their accomplishments during their tenure. A crowning achievement frequently defines their career. Yet, Dr. Maya Angelou famously said, "People will forget what you said, people will forget what you did, but they will never forget how you made them feel." Reflect on your own experiences. What stands out when you think about the best leaders throughout your life? You might recall some of their achievements, but more likely, you remember how they inspired you and made you feel.

Servant Leaders understand the link between their legacy and the emotions they create in others. They lead in a way that makes people feel valued and respected. They aim to challenge and support their teams, creating environments where optimism and joy outweigh negativity. They know not every moment under their leadership will be a kumbaya-singing hug-fest, but they strive to leave a positive impression overall.

So, how do you want to be remembered when your leadership role ends? This is an essential question to guide your daily actions. Are you creating conditions where people feel how you want them to feel about you? If the answer is yes, your leadership legacy is on the right track.

SERVING THE PERSON

"There is no greater gift you can give someone than your undivided attention."

— Jim Rohn

6

THE NEED TO BE SEEN

It's 8:00 a.m. on a construction job site. Joe, the site foreman, is discussing the day's plan with his crew. They'd talked with the superintendent the night before about today's tasks, but now a few details are unclear. "Not a problem," Joe says. "I'll connect with the superintendent and clarify. Has anyone seen him around?" The team members exchange glances, shrugging their shoulders. "Haven't seen him since early this morning," one worker offers. "Okay," Joe replies, "maybe Keith, the project manager, can help." At this, the team bursts into laughter. "Good luck with that," a worker quips. "He's in his trailer, buried in emails and calls, like always." Lacking direction, Joe hesitates to proceed. The work halts for over an hour until they track down the needed information.

Across town, at a biotechnology start-up, Mark, the company's Founder & CEO, is talking with his Chief Scientific Officer, Janet. "Keep me up to date on our progress. I'll be in Chicago and then Seattle through Friday this week," Mark explains. Janet sighs, visibly drained. "Mark," she says, "may I give you some feedback?" Mark nods hesitantly, knowing that Janet always speaks candidly. "This is your third trip this month," Janet begins, "and these next few days are critical for our testing. We all realize our partnerships are essential, and you're fantastic at managing relationships. But we need you here this week. Our team joined this company because they believe in you and our mission. Your energy carries us during demanding times like this.

With everyone anxious about the results, your presence and leadership will be invaluable."

Mark pauses, taken aback. He knows Janet is right. This week in the lab is pivotal, but his partner meetings feel equally vital. Janet, though brilliant, lacks Mark's ability to motivate the team. "I get it," Mark concedes. "But I can't be everywhere at once." Janet smiles. "Well, we can't clone you, and we don't have the budget for new execs. The question is: where is your leadership needed most?"

Your presence is a gift when you're in a leadership role. It may sound obvious—" showing up" is Leadership 101. Yet, leaders can't be everywhere, so presence management is critical. In the whirlwind of tasks, it's easy to lose sight of the people performing the work. However, the most fundamental workplace need is to be seen—especially by leaders.

What Does It Mean to Be Seen?

Being seen means having your presence, identity, emotions, and needs acknowledged. Leader acknowledgment can take many forms: validation, support, or inclusion. While we may not notice when this need is being met, we tend to immediately notice when we are not feeling seen. Feeling unseen can make us feel invisible, unnecessary, or neglected—nothing is more demoralizing than a leader who makes us feel this way. Unfortunately, this happens more often than it should, even with well-intentioned leaders.

A significant culprit is technology. In trying to boost communication and efficiency, we've created hyperconnected environments that paradoxically feel isolating. Leaders are inundated with emails, texts, video calls, Slack messages, and notifications. Tied to their desks and smartphones, leaders never fully disconnect. The incessant dings and chimes demand they address one crisis after another. This leaves little room for real human connection. Writer Linda Stone coined the term "continuous partial attention" to describe this phenomenon, and it's only gotten worse since the late 1980s when she observed it.

> **"We've stretched our attention bandwidth to upper limits. We think if technology has a lot of bandwidth, then we do, too. With continuous partial attention, we keep the top-level item in focus and scan the periphery in case something more important emerges. To be busy and connected is to feel alive. But the consequence is that we're over-stimulated, over-wound, unfulfilled."**
>
> *- Linda Stone (Former VP, Microsoft)*

This is why I say that attention is the currency of leadership today. Servant Leaders know that they have limited attention to invest, so they treat their time and presence as a savvy mutual fund manager would trade their stocks. To make the best investments, leaders need a sound strategy.

Investing Your Attention

"Where is my leadership needed the most right now?" This is a powerful question every leader should ask themselves regularly. Think of it as a micro-intervention amid the chaos. While immediate problems demand attention, they may not represent the highest leadership priorities. To determine where your presence will have the greatest impact, ask:

- Who is struggling with a problem? Invest in them by offering guidance.
- Who is facing a high-stakes moment? Invest in them by showing belief in their abilities.
- Who haven't you connected with recently? Reinvest in that relationship.
- Who is exceeding expectations? Invest in acknowledging their efforts.
- Who is experiencing emotional distress? Invest in offering to support them.
- Who belongs to an underserved minority group and may feel unseen? Invest in ensuring equal attention.
- Who holds little formal power but contributes significantly? Invest in validating their importance.

Notice that these questions focus on *who* rather than *what* is the priority?

Remember *Principle #1 – Mission First, People Always* when prioritizing your attention. Many leaders focus on task accomplishment, and caring for people becomes an afterthought. Servant Leaders know better. They assess where their presence and attention will have the most significant impact, and that's often caring for their greatest resource, their people.

Enhancing Approachability

Being seen is a two-way street. Leaders must not only direct attention toward their team but also create opportunities for their team to seek them out. This is why enhancing approachability is vitally important. An approachable leader is welcoming, friendly, and easy to talk to. They are also genuine, humble, and transparent. We approach them because they make us feel safe, valued, and respected. If you've experienced this kind of approachability in a leader firsthand, you know how inspiring it can be!

Contrast this with unapproachable leaders. They seem distant, busy, or intimidating. Team members may hesitate to approach them, assuming, "They don't have time for me" or "They won't care about my concerns." These assumptions are born from observations and experiences. Perhaps they've observed their leader's tendency to show impatience, stress, or emotional detachment. Or maybe their experience is one of "all business," where they feel unsafe sharing personal concerns with their leader. These cues speak volumes in terms of a leader's approachability.

How approachable are you as a leader? It's worth reflecting on. Many leaders I coach have an inflated sense of their approachability. They say, "I consistently smile and ask people how they are doing. People should feel very comfortable approaching me." However, genuine approachability is much more than looking cheery and making (often inauthentic) gestures of interest in how someone is feeling. Remember that approachable leaders make us feel safe enough to let our guard down and open up. But how do they do that? Let's address the things they <u>don't do</u> first. It's difficult to approach:

- Excitable, moody, inconsistent, or unpredictable leaders
- Highly critical, negative, and skeptical leaders
- Overly direct, harsh, and insensitive leaders

- Withdrawn and unresponsive leaders
- Arrogant, self-important, or entitled leaders
- Perfectionists or micro-managing leaders

Notice that these "don't do" behaviors exacerbate the power dynamic between leader and follower. That's because only a person in authority can license themselves to act this way and get away with it. Leaders often fail to understand that when in a role of formal authority, they are always wearing an invisible badge. Like police officers wear on their uniforms, the badge distinguishes them from regular citizens and validates their power. Think about when your boss is around you. Do you act a little differently? Most of us are more buttoned-up and careful with how we present ourselves. Even if we trust our manager, we act a little differently when interacting with peers or subordinates. Servant Leaders understand the power gap and how it works against their approachability. They make themselves more approachable by humbling themselves, meeting people where they are, and relating to their experiences.

The Physical Environment

Your physical environment can also signal approachability—or lack thereof. Let's start with a leader's physical appearance. Organizational culture dictates what's appropriate, and how you dress needs to correspond with your role. Yet, more senior leaders might benefit from dressing slightly more casually to appear less intimidating. But don't overdo it! People can get the wrong perception if you try to be overly humble or easygoing. I once coached an executive in a tech startup who received negative feedback for wearing hip t-shirts and flashy sneakers. He felt he was being authentic and enhancing his approachability. However, the incongruence between his role expectations and appearance created mistrust, not connection. Even in a trendy startup culture, a leader should appear well-groomed, professional and exude presence. e

Similarly, your workspace should feel welcoming. Is it comfortable and inviting? Does it provide insight into your personal life outside of work? If you work in an office, do you mostly keep your door open or closed? Ensure your desk is not an obstacle when people enter your space. Move it to the side so people can access you directly. Strategically place a chair for guests that forces you to focus on them rather than your computer screen. Your workspace should signal, "I'm available and will give you my attention."

More people work from home now, so their home office background becomes equally important. A warm and inviting virtual background is good, but a real background with visible artifacts expressing your personality is even better. Pictures of family, dogs, or anything that might be a conversation starter make you relatable. Also, be mindful of your camera quality and lighting. It's hard enough to read non-verbal communication through a screen, so dark and fuzzy pictures don't help. People who struggle to assess your emotions are less likely to feel safe approaching you.

Connecting through Conversation

The most approachable leaders are master conversationalists. They create authentic, meaningful dialogue with everyone, from executives to entry-level staff. One of my favorite examples involves one of my coaching clients. He was a retired military officer who transitioned to executive leadership in a Fortune 500—let's call him Jim. He was in charge of several thousand people and had enormous P&L responsibility. Yet, Jim made time to consistently walk the floor and chat about his love for the New York Jets and Italian food with his foreman. His people loved him because he wasn't leading from an ivory tower; he was just "Jim from Long Island." Equally impressive was how the C-Suite officers thought of Jim. They told me, "Jim is masterful in the boardroom. He knows his audience, their pain points, and how to create meaningful dialogue." Jim clearly excelled at connecting through conversation at all levels.

How do guys like Jim do it? While personality traits like high extroversion, sociability, and interpersonal sensitivity help, anyone can learn to be a better conversationalist. It starts with creating the space for authentic conversation to exist. If co-located with your team in an office environment, make time for "leadership by walking around." This is simply visiting others in their own space and engaging in informal conversation to gain insight and strengthen relationships.

I can get pushback from leaders who are less naturally inclined toward conversation. They tell me, "That seems disruptive and could get awkward. What do I say to them?" I understand the hesitancy, so I created the following guide to help them out. I call these sorts of interactions "Check-In Chats." These informal, 5-15-minute interactions allow leaders to build rapport without derailing their schedules. While they mainly support impromptu in-person conversations, remote teams can also benefit from structured time for personal exchanges during virtual meetings. Try starting your next virtual meeting with, "What was the best piece of advice you ever received?" Or "If you could visit any country in the world, where would you go?" Get over any reservations you have about this level of informality and try it out. Check-in Chats and fun questions during virtual meetings are a small investment of time, but the impact on trust and connection is profound.

Check-in Chats – How Leaders Build Rapport

1. **Must Be Present to Win** - Just like a raffle ticket, you can't win if you are not in the room when the ticket's drawn. It's more important to be consistent than to be perfect with your dialogue. Trust is built over time.
2. **Set the Tone** – Explain your intent. You don't want to talk about tasks; you are there to learn and connect.
3. **Be Positive** – A great way to open up a conversation is to bring them some good news and share examples of good work/success.
4. **Small Talk is a Big Deal** – What was the best part of your weekend? Did you catch the game last night? Share insights about your family, hobbies, and passions. Being vulnerable allows them to do the same with you.
5. **Pulse Check** - Ask, "What is working well right now?" Then follow up with "What is not working well right now?" Ask them to share authentically. Avoid criticizing, judging, or interrupting. Simply listen.
6. **Practice Open Body Language** – Never cross arms or have hands on hips. Ensure eye contact, head nods, open posture, and appropriate facial gestures (smiling, etc.)
7. **Sweat the Small Stuff** – Empathize with their challenges and commit to helping/supporting them if you can.

8. **Share Your Experiences** – Leaders often have experiences and insights that others do not. Share knowledge through coaching, mentoring, and storytelling.
9. **Share Your Vision** – People feel connected to their work when they understand the bigger picture. Communicate the team's direction and their role in success.
10. **Have fun**! – People are often drawn to leaders who have a sense of humor. If you have that gift, show your lighter side and appropriately joke around some.

Self-Management & Approachability

Finally, a leader's capacity for managing emotions significantly impacts their approachability. If you recall from *Principle #2 – Character Defines Your Destiny*, the "D" in our character equation stands for "Discipline," specifically the ability to manage difficult emotions. Nothing makes us feel more unsafe than a leader expressing unfiltered negative emotions. We all get how an excitable leader who yells can alienate people. But this is becoming less acceptable in today's workplaces, so it's not as common. What I observe more these days are leaders who think they are doing well at managing their emotions, but they wear them on their sleeves. They think they are masking their anger, disappointment, and stress, but everyone around them knows exactly how they feel.

"You can't control how you feel, but you can always choose the way you act."

- Mel Robbins (New York Times Bestselling author)

Managing emotions verbally and nonverbally when in a leadership position is imperative. As someone whose personality is dispositioned for extremes, I've spent a lifetime working on this. I created my "Choice Gap" Model for Emotional Regulation to help leaders pause and reframe their responses to challenging situations.

Expanding Your Choice Gap for Emotional Regulation

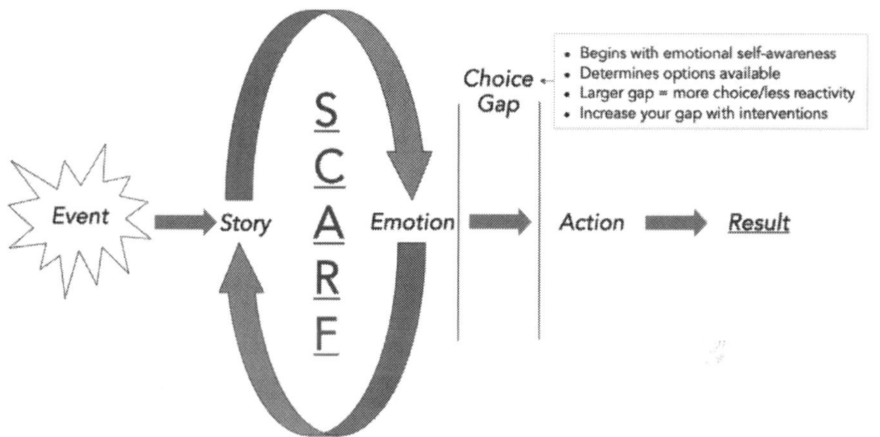

Missed expectations concerning: Status, Certainty, Autonomy, Relatedness, and Fairness = Fear/Anger

Here's how it works: When you observe an event, you experience an emotion, then apply a story to explain what is happening to you. The emotion and your story happen almost simultaneously, feeding one another. The emotional story determines the actions available to you. You then choose an action that produces results. Undesirable results usually occur when we are feeling negative emotions. The key to getting better results is expanding your Choice Gap, which is the space between emotion and taking action.

Easier said than done, though! The first step is becoming more aware of your emotions and recognizing how they influence the stories you tell yourself. Neuroleadership expert David Rock uses the acronym SCARF to explain how humans react to threats and rewards: Status, Certainty, Autonomy, Relatedness, and Fairness. If your interpretation of an event suggests you've lost status, perceive the future as uncertain, feel your autonomy is compromised, struggle to relate to your team, or view a situation as unfair, negative emotions like fear or anger will likely emerge.[11] These emotions often drive us to act in ways that don't serve us as leaders. While you can't stop yourself from creating a narrative or experiencing negative emotions, you can learn to pause and slow your reaction, creating space for a more thoughtful response.

Now, you are ready to implement an intervention strategy and gain a fresh perspective. What are these magical intervention strategies, you might ask? Among the various approaches to emotional regulation, the cognitive reappraisal strategy stands out as my favorite. Dr. James Gross, a psychologist and expert in emotional regulation at Stanford University, defines cognitive reappraisals as the "attempt to reinterpret an emotion-eliciting situation in a way that alters its meaning and changes its emotional impact."[12] Simply put, it's about rewriting the story in your head to create a more empowering narrative. It helps to have a set of ready-to-use reappraisal strategies to reframe your perspective successfully. Here are a few examples:

- **Long Run Strategy** – "In ten years' time, how might I see this?"
- **Normalizing Strategy** – "It's okay for me to feel this way, given the situation."
- **Best Case Strategy** – "Can I visualize the best possible outcome?"
- **Legacy Strategy** – "How do I want to be remembered as a leader?"
- **Empathy Strategy** – "Can I step into their shoes and understand why they may be acting this way?"

Here is an illustration of how it works:

Scenario - You check in with one of your direct reports, and they haven't completed a task to the standard you were expecting from them. You are now behind schedule, and your mind creates a story for why this happened. Your report didn't listen to you, and he lacks focus! This will cause the team to work extra hours this evening to meet a pressing deadline. Your story feeds emotions of frustration and stress. However, you notice your negative emotions and smartly insert the "Long Run" reappraisal strategy. This gives you additional perspective and decreases your reactivity. You now have the space to act more in alignment with who you want to be as a leader.

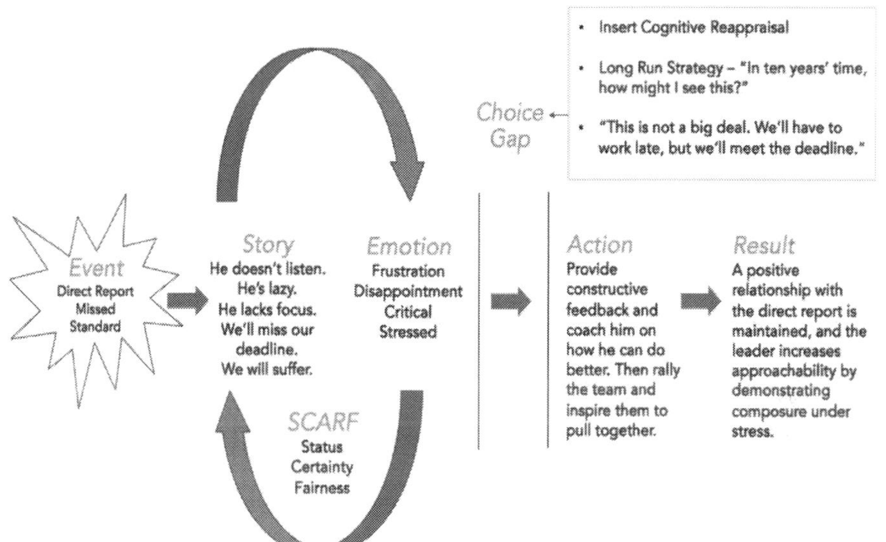

If the original stories and emotions guided your actions, you would likely act in a way that hurt your approachability. By inserting the reappraisal strategy, you can self-manage and produce a better result. The day your people stop approaching you is the day you stop leading them! However, no leader can always be at their best, and experiencing negative emotions is unavoidable. Servant Leaders prepare for these moments by always keeping a reappraisal strategy in their back pocket and intervening when necessary.

Serving the Need to Be Seen

Meeting the Need to Be Seen is foundational for Servant Leaders. In our hyper-connected world, leaders are more distracted than ever, and attention is the new currency of leadership. By consistently asking, "Who needs my attention most right now?" and showing up authentically, leaders build trust and connection. Practice enhancing your approachability as well. Ensure your presence signals safety and become a master conversationalist. When people feel seen, valued, and safe, high performance becomes not just possible but inevitable.

Self-Assess

How well do you "invest your attention" on a daily basis?

1-----------2------------3------------4------------5------------6------------7

The days biggest fire usually gets most of my attention

I focus my day on *who* rather than *what* is the priority

How would your team rate your accessibility and availability?

1-----------2------------3------------4------------5------------6------------7

I can be difficult to access and have limited availability

I'm available anytime, no matter how busy I get

How well do you know the people that you lead?

1-----------2------------3------------4------------5------------6------------7

The minimum amount, we talk about work

Particularly well, to include knowing personal details

How well do you manage difficult emotions in the workplace?

1-----------2------------3------------4------------5------------6------------7

I verbally/nonverbally let people know exactly how I feel

I manage negative emotions and avoid reactivity

Scoring:

24-28 = Congrats! Your team likely feels seen

13-23 = People mostly feel seen on your team, but there's still work to do

4-12 = Being seen may be an underserved need on your team

Reflect

Where is your leadership needed the most right now? Where do you need to be present and invest your attention?

What could you practice to better connect with people during conversations?

Which cognitive reappraisal strategy will you keep in your back pocket for the next time you feel a difficult emotion?

Recap

- Presence is power. Where you show up—and how you show up—shapes culture and performance.
- Attention is today's leadership currency. Invest it in people, not just problems.
- Approachability matters. Your energy, appearance, and environment send signals about your openness.
- Check-in Chats build connection. Informal, consistent conversations make people feel valued and safe.
- Self-management expands your impact. Regulate emotions with intention to become a leader others trust.
- Pause, then lead. Expand your "Choice Gap" to respond thoughtfully instead of reacting impulsively.
- When people feel seen, they show up fully. And when leaders prioritize this need, they don't just manage people—they inspire them.

7

THE NEED TO BE HEARD

In the spring of 2020, the world faced unprecedented challenges in maintaining productivity while navigating the pandemic. Many of my clients struggled, and my business nearly ground to a halt as training events were indefinitely suspended. One client, for whom I had recently rolled out a year-long training program for high-potential leaders, hit the pause button and joined the great work-from-home experiment. For some employees, the absence of a commute and the freedom to work in their pajamas were welcome changes. For others, the isolation became suffocating. Disconnection set in, and productivity steadily declined.

In June, the CEO called me and said, "We've got to do something different. I need you to put together a virtual training program on how to lead remotely." I took on the challenge, partnering with a colleague who had extensive experience managing remote teams. Together, we identified best practices for leading remotely and crafted a series of webinars with practical content and exercises. We were proud of what we built, and we rolled it out later that month.

The program was a big success, but not for the reasons we expected. While participants found the content useful, they most appreciated the opportunity to connect with their peers and senior leaders. Morale had plummeted, and employees craved a space to express their challenges. They wanted to be heard!

Though many problems were beyond anyone's control, it was cathartic for them to share their feelings and discover that others felt the same.

Following this revelation, my partner and I redesigned the webinars to include more breakout room time and refocused some of the content to train leaders on how to ensure their teams felt heard. The impact was profound. The leadership team's commitment to addressing the organization's need to be heard transformed morale and productivity. The company's bottom line was astonishingly strong by year-end, especially given the year's economic turmoil.

One of the most fundamental yet powerful human needs is the need to be heard. It goes hand in hand with the need to be seen. Once we feel safe, accessible, and acknowledged by our leaders, we yearn to express ourselves—to share our ideas, feelings, and experiences. On the surface, this sharing might seem transactional—proposing an idea to improve efficiency or flagging a challenge to garner support. But beneath it lies an unconscious desire for acknowledgment, validation, and appreciation. When a leader makes us feel heard, it boosts our self-esteem and strengthens our sense of value, inspiring loyalty and deepening relationships.

Conversely, being disregarded—having our voices go unheard—is profoundly demoralizing. Think about how it feels to speak up and be ignored. Frustration, exclusion, insignificance, rejection, and even resentment can quickly set in. Reread those emotions and feel the energy. Do they sound conducive to high performance? Certainly not.

Servant Leaders recognize this and strive to ensure their people feel heard. Addressing this need fosters acceptance and optimism, replacing negative emotions with those that fuel productivity and engagement. While this may sound more like therapy than leadership, the results speak for themselves. Helping others feel heard drives better outcomes—and that's what great leaders prioritize.

How to Listen Like a Leader

Servant Leadership demands exceptional listening skills. Unfortunately, many leaders mistakenly believe they're already good listeners when they're often not. The truth is that effective listening requires intention, energy, and discipline—qualities that often falter under the weight of leadership responsibilities.

Two significant barriers to effective listening are energy and authority. First, good listening is mentally exhausting. Try giving someone your undivided attention for an hour, and you'll feel it. I limit my coaching calls to three daily because I know my physical limits. Leaders, however, often push through long days, and their ability to listen diminishes as their energy wanes.

Second, leaders' formal authority often places them in "transmit mode" instead of "receive mode." If you've ever talked on a two-way radio, you know that only one person can transmit at a time. The transmission's receiver must listen and wait for the transmitter to finish before responding. When broadcasting their message, leaders can forget to switch to receiving and give others airtime. Overcoming these challenges begins with being fully present.

Getting Fully Present

"Getting present" is a popular phrase in today's world of information overload, but it's not easy to achieve. Leaders often find their minds pulled in three directions: ruminating on the past, pseudo-listening to the present, and anticipating the future. This mental multitasking causes them to miss details, connections, and emotional cues, leaving the speaker feeling unheard.

> **"Directing attention toward where it needs to go is a primal task of leadership."**
>
> *- Daniel Goleman, Focus: The Hidden Driver of Excellence.*

Directing your attention to the present moment is challenging but achievable through deliberate practice. It starts with greater mindfulness and noticing when your attention drifts. The goal is not to stop your mind from wandering. If you've ever meditated, you know that trying to stop your thoughts from happening is a surefire way to ensure they persist! Instead, acknowledge your thoughts without judgment and allow them to pass. Then, gently refocus. When you notice you are fully present and in the "here and now," you've centered yourself.

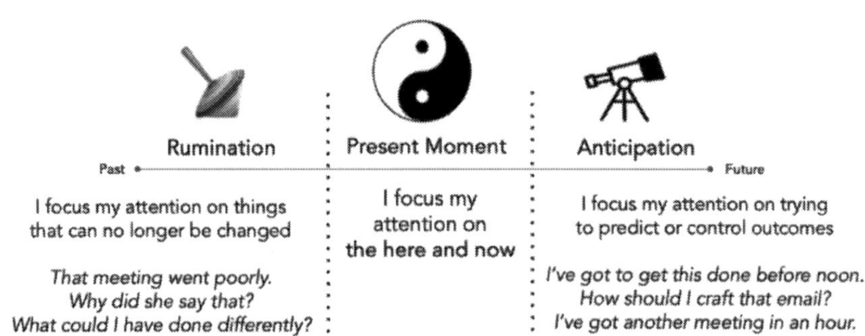

My favorite technique for centering oneself is the one-minute body scan. This micro-meditation brings your attention to your body and breath, helping you reset and refocus. Here's how it works:

The Body Scan – (1 Minute) Micro-Mediation

1. Sit comfortably in a chair and close your eyes or gaze softly at the floor.
2. Notice your **feet**. Bring your attention to your toes and trace your attention back to your heel. Feel the weight of your feet making contact with the ground.
3. Notice your **spine**. Walk your attention up the back of your legs and rest it at the base of your spine. Now, trace it up your spine and stop when you reach your shoulders. If there is tension in your shoulders, try to release it.
4. Notice your **hands**. See if you can feel the air in between your fingers.
5. Notice your **breath**. Observe as your body inhales into your lungs and exhales over your lips. Allow three breaths to unfold.

Tip: You don't have to memorize this entirely at first. Use the prompt "I have feet, a spine, hands, and I breathe." With enough practice, you will begin to remember the details.

Once you finish your body scan, open your eyes and notice how you feel. You should feel calmer, clearer, and ready to listen fully. I've shared this technique with many executives who have reported great success. It's simple yet transformative.

You Never Learned to Listen

Now that you're present and prepared to listen, let's dive into maximizing the skills to help people feel genuinely heard. What do you think those skills are? It's surprisingly difficult to put into words. The irony is that while listening is one of the most crucial life skills, most of us were never formally taught how to do it well. Unless you're a therapist or coach, your knowledge of listening is likely cobbled together from "on-the-job training." It's time to elevate your listening game by understanding a few critical techniques.

To begin, let's discuss what it means to be an active listener. There are some known challenges that get in the way of our ability to listen to someone else. One challenge is that we have our own emotional needs and want to get them met. Leaders often want to appear helpful and valuable, so to get that need met, we take on a problem to solve. Solving problems reflects well on us, and that makes us feel good. Active listening is suspending your own emotional needs and listening to what's being said instead of problem-solving. Perhaps they only want to share their experience with you! I hear this a lot from engineering clients and coupled friends. The feedback they receive is, "I don't need you to solve my problem for me. I just want to talk about it!"

Another challenge is that as we listen, we tend to relate everything to our own experiences. While this can help us empathize, it often leads us astray. We may start hearing someone's story about a co-worker undermining them and immediately recall a similar experience we had. Suddenly, their narrative becomes filtered through our own lens, and we begin coloring their story with meaning that might not align with their reality. Active listening means noticing when this happens and choosing to remain focused on their experience. No matter how much you think you understand someone else's feelings, remember that each person experiences things uniquely.

The final challenge is listening to understand versus to respond. Picture this: someone is speaking, and they say something that resonates with you. You've experienced it before, so you know exactly where they're going with things. As they continue talking, your mind races ahead, formulating your response. The voice in your head is now saying, "Okay, I got it; hurry up and finish so I can tell you what I think!" You've tuned out and likely started missing key details. Active listening requires staying out of your head and fully engaging with the person in front of you. It means resisting the temptation to shape their story before they've finished sharing.

The Power of Nonverbal Cues

Listening isn't just about what's said but also about what's unsaid. Studies suggest that 65-96% of communication is nonverbal. Leaders must pay close attention to what they observe and the nonverbal signals they send in return. Eye contact, for example, is one of the most powerful indicators of active listening. Not prolonged staring that makes people uncomfortable, but natural, three-to-five-second glances that convey attention. A well-timed nod or facial expression—like a smile at something lighthearted or raised eyebrows at a surprise—also demonstrates engagement.

Equally important is noticing others' nonverbal cues, particularly those that reveal emotions. People won't always explicitly tell you they're frustrated or disappointed, but their body language—a low tone, clenched jaw, or furrowed brow—speaks volumes. These cues become even more critical when there's a disconnect between verbal and nonverbal communication. For example, someone might say, "I'm on board with your decision," while their body language suggests the opposite. Missing these signals means missing vital information.

Techniques for Active Listening

To truly excel at listening, consider incorporating three powerful techniques: rephrasing, open-ended questions, and labeling emotions.

1. **Rephrasing** - Rephrasing involves restating what you've heard to confirm understanding. For example, you might say, "So, I'm hearing that you and Mark were debating how to get the project back on track, and you

felt he was prioritizing his team's resources over collaboration." Adding, "That's disappointing because he's normally a team player," shows empathy and validates their feelings. Rephrasing demonstrates that you're tracking details and allows the speaker to clarify or expand their thoughts.

Some people think rephrasing sounds robotic or like "management speak." The trick is to make it authentic to your style. Instead of saying, "So, what I'm hearing is...," try:

- "Quick check-in—I understand you were trying to get the schedule back on track..."
- "Let me make sure I've got this right. You're saying..."
- "Ok, so you were talking with Mark about the schedule and..."

Adjust the language to feel natural for you while ensuring clarity.

2. **Open-Ended Questions** - Open-ended questions deepen the conversation. Unlike yes-or-no questions, they invite richer responses. Consider this example:
   - **Closed-ended**: "Did you ask Mark why he acted that way?"
   - **Open-ended**: "Given the pressure both of you were under to meet the schedule, how did you handle it when he pushed back?"

   Open-ended questions show understanding, encourage reflection, and keep the dialogue moving.

3. **Labeling Emotions** - Too often, leaders get stuck in problem-solving mode and listen only to the surface-level facts being shared. Many leaders also try to compartmentalize emotions in the workplace or even ignore them. Servant Leaders see emotions as important data and listen for the "music beneath the words." Identifying and naming emotions validates the speaker like nothing else can. Using our example, instead of glossing over frustrations, you might say, "It sounds like you're feeling disappointed and maybe even a little hurt by how this played out with Mark."

   To sharpen this skill, expand your emotional vocabulary. Tools like the "Wheel of Emotions" can help you identify nuanced feelings. A leader who recognizes someone is not just "sad" but specifically "disappointed" or "embarrassed" demonstrates a deeper level of understanding.

The original version of the feeling wheel (with its six core feelings) was created by Dr. Gloria Willcox in 1982. Since then, there have been many adaptations as researchers and therapists have added their spin on it. Whenever I share this resource with my clients, they tend to react with surprise, awe, and overwhelm. They immediately realize how much work is needed to become emotionally literate and how important this skill is!

The Wheel of Emotions

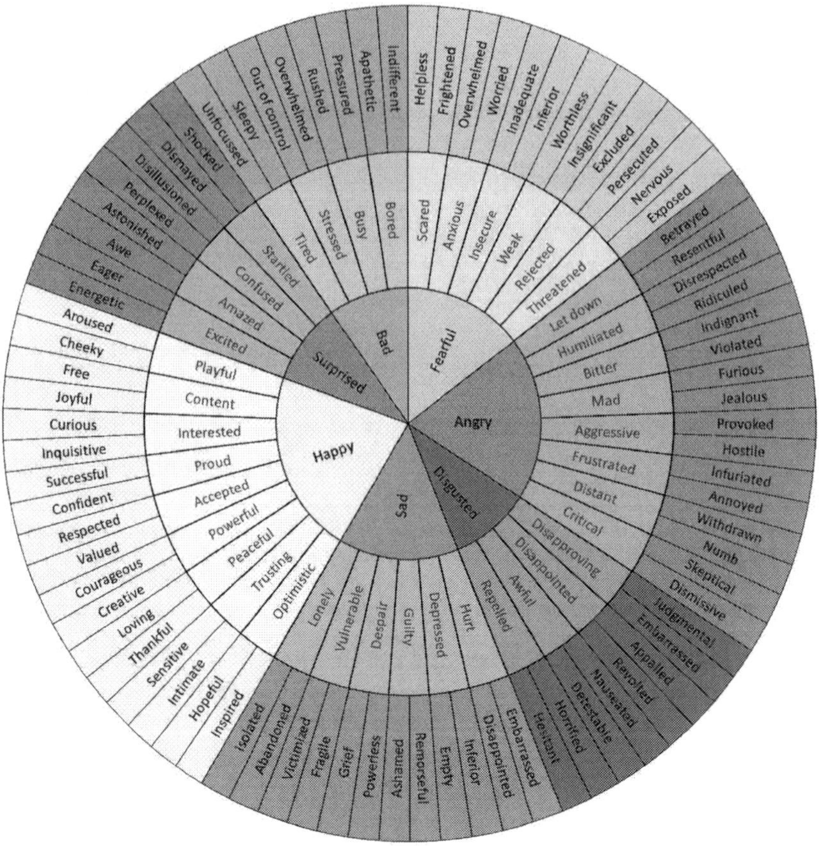

Download the full-size color version at www.davidspungin.com

Creating Space for Inclusive Dialogue

Even with strong listening skills, voices can still go unheard, especially in group settings. Group dynamics can impact a leader's self-awareness and reshape expectations of how they should interact. Leaders often unintentionally dominate team discussions, interrupt, or dismiss concerns. They fall into the trap of thinking their power and authority make their voices more relevant. I've coached many seasoned executives who think very fast and are habitual interrupters. They tell me, "I know where they are going with this, and I'm intervening to save everyone's time." They feel as if their interruption is a service to their team members! However, they make assumptions and do not fully understand their team members' reasoning. This results in team members feeling discounted and disempowered.

To avoid this, practice conversational patience. Instead of interjecting, imagine setting your response on a metaphorical table. Wait until the speaker has finished. You can always pick your response back up off the table. However, many leaders find their original response irrelevant because they hear new details that change their thinking.

> **"Big egos have little ears."**
>
> *- Robert Schuller, Pastor, Speaker, and Author*

Another critical question to consider is, "How do I handle challenges or disagreements?" If you become defensive or dismissive, your team will quickly learn not to voice dissent. Servant Leaders welcome respectful disagreement. They view feedback—even when uncomfortable—as an opportunity for growth. No leader likes being wrong, but it's better to be effective than "right." Effective leadership requires humility that invites criticism.

Set clear expectations for dissent by telling your team, "I expect you to speak your mind 100% of the time. If I make a mistake, I want you to call me out. Feedback helps all of us improve—including me." Note that you can't communicate this once and expect people to act on it. You must license the team to act this way by consistently communicating this expectation. Sooner or later, people will take you up on it and challenge or disagree with you. Know this is a critical moment, and how you respond will set the tone. Stay open and non-defensive. Your behavior will either build trust or erode it.

Finally, pay attention to power dynamics. Power imbalances often mean some voices—especially minority voices—are overlooked. Actively ensure all perspectives are heard. If a quieter team member hasn't spoken, invite them to share: "Yao, we haven't heard your perspective yet. What are your thoughts?" If someone is interrupted, redirect the conversation: "Let's hear Gabriella finish her point first, then we'll circle back." Group dynamics imbalances and one's willingness to engage within the team can manifest from many differences. Servant leaders will benefit from simply paying attention and being curious. Who is taking up all the airtime? Who is being included/not included? Why might that be? If your gut tells you things are going unsaid, create space for more inclusive dialogue to unfold. Missing voices are missed perspectives. And missed perspectives can lead to wasted opportunities at best, or crippling team dysfunction at worst. Be a Servant Leader who insists that all voices be heard, validated, and valued. Doing so will inspire deep respect and loyalty from those you serve.

Serving the Need to Be Heard

The second foundational need every Servant Leader must address is the *Need to Be Heard.* Serving this need requires exceptional listening skills. In today's distraction-filled world, it starts with a leader's ability to refocus on the present moment. From there, great leaders demonstrate active listening by rephrasing, asking open-ended questions, and naming emotions. Finally, they create space for inclusive dialogue, ensuring that every voice is valued. When people feel heard, they feel respected—and that respect establishes a foundation of trust and loyalty that fuels high performance.

Self-Assess

How skilled are you at getting present and directing attention?

1-----------2------------3------------4------------5------------6------------7

It's difficult for me to focus and not multitask

I live in the present moment & focus my attention

How well do you actively listen?

1-----------2------------3------------4------------5------------6------------7

I hear the facts and mostly listen to respond

I rephrase, ask smart questions, and observe non-verbal cues

How well do you notice emotions and can name them for others?

1-----------2------------3------------4------------5------------6------------7

Emotions are messy and not for the workplace

I am empathetic and have a large emotional vocabulary

How well do you encourage dialogue within your team?

1-----------2------------3------------4------------5------------6------------7

I tend to talk the most and can interrupt others

I encourage dissent and facilitate missing voices

Scoring:

24-28 = Congrats! Your team likely feels heard

13-23 = People mostly feel heard on your team, but there's still work to do

4-12 = Feeling heard may be an underserved need on your team

Reflect

When do you tend to feel uncentered and/or unfocused? In what situations do you find yourself unable to focus on the person in front of you?

What skills of active listening are you doing well already? What active listening skills could you use some additional work on?

What emotions are hard for you to notice and empathize with? What emotions are you able to notice and empathize with easily?

What members of your team don't get heard enough? How might you begin to include their voices more often?

Recap

- Being heard isn't just about surface-level communication—it meets a deep emotional need for validation, connection, and value.
- When people feel ignored or dismissed, they experience emotions like frustration, exclusion, or resentment, which undermine morale and performance.
- Active listening is a core skill of Servant Leadership. It requires energy, presence, and humility—especially when authority tempts leaders to dominate conversations.
- Key techniques for effective listening include:
  - Getting fully present through practices like the 1-minute body scan
  - Rephrasing to confirm understanding
  - Asking open-ended questions to invite deeper dialogue
  - Labeling emotions to acknowledge the speaker's experience
- Nonverbal cues are powerful; leaders must tune into both what's said and what's left unsaid.
- In group settings, strong leaders practice conversational patience, welcome dissent, and invite feedback—even when it's uncomfortable

SERVING THE WORK

"If your actions inspire others to dream more, learn more, do more, and become more, you are a leader."

— John Quincy Adams

8

THE NEED FOR AUTONOMY

"I'm sorry, I don't think I heard you correctly. Why am I being removed from my project?" Bill exclaimed, his disbelief evident. To him, it made no sense. Bill had amassed thirty years of experience managing complex, high-visibility projects. The multi-year, billion-dollar project he currently led was perfectly aligned with his expertise. Bill was always the company's go-to leadership choice if a project was particularly challenging or high-risk. He had spent his entire career cultivating this reputation. To be suddenly replaced as project lead felt like a punch to the gut.

"Bill, you're an excellent technical leader—one of our very best," the CEO began. "Your attention to detail, ability to forecast risks, and relentless commitment to results are highly valued. But I need to be frank: you're also a serious micromanager." The CEO continued, "The feedback from your team is consistent: they feel suffocated. You're controlling every project detail, leaving no room for them to breathe. They say you discount their ideas and get frustrated when they take initiative, often redoing their work yourself. It's not working, Bill."

Bill sat there, bewildered. "Maybe my style isn't for everyone," he countered, "but at the end of the day, I get results. Better than anyone else."

"Yes, your results look great on paper—if we're measuring performance by KPIs alone," the CEO responded. "But there's more to leadership than hitting targets. How many junior leaders have left your projects over the last five years?"

"I don't know…a few," Bill admitted.

"It's more than a few," the CEO said firmly. "Six high-potential leaders left under your watch. They all had enormous promise, and our competitors quickly scooped them up. Their exit interviews cited a lack of leadership and growth as their primary reasons for leaving. We can't keep bleeding top talent like this."

Bill's arms crossed defensively. "Those people had other reasons for leaving, too. That's not fair."

"Bill, most of them said they weren't growing under your leadership," the CEO continued. "You not only micromanaged them, but you also bypassed them and micromanaged *their* teams. Think about it: how many leaders from your team have been promoted? How many are positioned to take over your role someday? Careers on your projects tend to stagnate. And right now, we have several 'rockstar' leaders on this team who need a mentor who will take their development to the next level. We no longer believe you're the right person to lead them."

This fictitious story is based on conditions that led me to coach Bill. When I first started working with him, he was devastated. But to his credit, he was open to learning and growing from the experience. Part of the problem was that Bill had never received the feedback he needed to adjust. As a senior leader with power and authority, his team was too intimidated to share their honest feelings.

I gathered candid feedback, helping Bill process the impact of his management style. Together, we worked on increasing his flexibility and transitioning from a micromanager to a strategic leader. He learned to provide less direction and more facilitation, shifting his identity from "problem solver" to "coach." Over time, Bill cultivated a team culture where autonomy and initiative were valued and rewarded. Today, his people love working on his projects, and Bill embodies the essence of a Servant Leader.

Autonomy's Link to Motivation

We intuitively understand the importance of autonomy because we've experienced it firsthand. Think back to your teenage years—those pivotal moments when you began craving independence from your parents. Choosing your friends, clothes, music, and activities was part of forming your identity. You transitioned from being someone else's child to becoming your own person. Exercising autonomy wasn't just something you *wanted*—it was critical to your development.

How much did you personally crave autonomy at eighteen? I remember being fiercely independent, eager to "fly the nest" and start my own life. Now, as a parent of teenagers, I'm watching this unfold with my own kids. They think they are already adults, wrestling daily to prove it to us and the world. Being an adult, however, isn't easy. It requires sacrifice, responsibility, and sound decision-making—qualities that aren't always as fun as the carefree days of childhood. Yet, my teenagers persist because strong internal forces drive their desire for autonomy.

This drive for independence is deeply embedded in our DNA. Autonomy helps us form our sense of self, survive without dependency, and thrive. The more control we have over our decisions, the more enthusiastic and invested we become. Autonomy fosters ownership, sparks creativity, and fuels innovation. When we make decisions and see positive outcomes, we feel a sense of accomplishment and fulfillment. Over time, these experiences contribute to greater confidence and emotional well-being.

So, if autonomy is such a powerful motivator—universally desired and deeply beneficial—why aren't workplaces more empowered?

The Dilemma of Empowerment

We all want to be self-directed and have control over our work. This is why companies emphasize "empowering" teams as part of effective leadership. However, these same companies also demand accountability for results, and autonomous team members with little oversight can be a recipe for disaster. This creates a classic "chicken-or-egg" dilemma: Leaders empower people they trust, yet trust can't be earned unless people are given opportunities to prove themselves. As leaders weigh risks, unproductive mindsets often emerge, preventing them from letting go.

Shifting to an Empowerment Mindset

Leaders often struggle to relinquish control, especially when they're held accountable for results. Who can blame them? Leadership is unforgiving. Meet expectations, and you keep your job—maybe earn a promotion. Fail to deliver results, and the company will find someone else who can.

The weight of accountability makes it easy to justify *not* delegating. Over the years, I've worked with thousands of leaders to uncover the unproductive mindsets holding them back from empowering their teams. Here are the most consistent themes:

1. **"They don't know how to do it right."**
   You assume others lack the experience to succeed, so you'll have to redo their work. But "right" is subjective. Just because someone takes a different path doesn't mean it's wrong. Focus on results, not the process.

2. **"They'll take too long, and I don't have time to help."**
   Yes, delegation requires an upfront investment of time. But it's a long-term strategy. Building new capabilities today creates efficiencies tomorrow.

3. **"I can't influence the outcome."**
   True—and that's the point. Empowering others frees you to focus on higher-level priorities. You can't scale yourself without letting go.

4. **"They're too busy. I don't want to burden them."**
   This mindset masquerades as empathy but masks deeper fears, like losing control. Trust your team to manage their workload.

5. **"I won't be as valuable or relevant."**
   This self-preservation mindset always backfires. True leaders achieve results *through* others, not by doing everything themselves. Leaders who can't delegate are less valuable and are rarely promoted.

6. **"My reputation is on the line. I can't afford mistakes."**
   When you empower people, they will make some mistakes. This is unavoidable. But mistakes are opportunities to learn and grow. If your people are "failing forward," you're building long-term resilience and

competence. Having a reputation as a people developer is more valuable than being an individual problem-solver.

By now, you've likely embraced the idea that meeting an individual's need for autonomy can be a powerful intrinsic motivator. You've also recognized the importance of shifting mindsets to practice more outstanding delegation and empowerment. Let's now delve into specific best practices and tactics Servant Leaders can use to empower their teams.

Using Commander's Intent

What comes to mind when you hear the phrase "military style of leadership"? Many people imagine commanding officers barking orders at soldiers with strict adherence to a rigid chain of command. Hollywood often reinforces this stereotype of centralized, inflexible control. However, the reality is quite different. The U.S. military, for instance, is one of the most empowered organizations in the world. While respecting rank and obeying lawful orders matter, decision-making is often decentralized—and for good reason. Combat is chaotic. Intricate plans are frequently rendered obsolete as soon as the fighting begins. The saying goes, "No plan survives first contact because the enemy always has a vote."

In this environment, command-and-control leadership simply doesn't work. It's too slow, and decision-makers are often too far removed from the reality on the frontlines. By the time information travels up the chain of command, it's outdated. To address this, the U.S. military employs intent-based orders, which always begin with an overarching vision called Commander's Intent. This vision guides decision-making when plans fall apart or orders are delayed.

Commander's Intent is the ultimate empowerment tool. It's essentially saying, "Here's my idea. I know things won't go exactly as planned, so I trust you to figure out how to make it happen." While vital in battle, this approach is equally valuable in business. Let's explore the three components of the **Commander's Intent framework—Purpose, Key Tasks, and End State**—and how to apply them effectively.

Purpose – Why are we doing this?

The Purpose component answers the "why" behind a task or objective. While this may seem straightforward, many leaders overlook the opportunity to explain why something is important. Instead, they focus solely on tasks, assuming that's what matters most. Some leaders even argue, "No one really has time to sit around and always explain why we are doing things." However, investing time in sharing the purpose will yield big dividends. When people understand the why, their efforts take on meaning, and they feel more valuable. Purpose fosters initiative and intrinsic motivation, enabling team members to make decisions without constant supervision. Here's an example:

Sales Manager: *"I need you to deliver a presentation to a potential client next month on our capabilities.* ***The purpose is to convince them that we have the fastest technology available to meet their needs so we can close the deal by the end of the quarter."***

Sales Rep: *"Got it. I'll start this week and have a draft ready by next Friday."*

Later that week, the Federal Reserve increased interest rates, the stock market tumbled, and a potential recession looms. The Sales Manager and Rep sit down together the following Friday to review the draft.

Sales Manager: *"Thanks for your hard work on this presentation. Let's see what you've pulled together."*

Sales Rep: *"Sure. Originally, I laid out specifically how our technology will speed up their decision-making and increase productivity. However, since we would like to close a deal this quarter, I decided to refocus our value proposition more on how higher productivity will lead to greater cost savings. You can really feel people's concerns right now about the economy, and I believe reducing costs will be top of mind for them this quarter."*

The Sales Rep demonstrated initiative and ownership by understanding the purpose, delivering a more relevant and effective presentation. Wouldn't it be great if everyone on your team showed this kind of initiative? Of course it would! You hire talented people for a reason. You want critical thinkers who can operate autonomously within your intentions. Thoughtfully sharing purpose is a crucial first step to making this happen.

Key Tasks – What must we do to succeed?

Key Tasks outline the critical actions required for success. In the military, standardized terms like "feint," "ambush," or "defend in sector" have distinctive meanings and various subtasks associated with them. Officers and NCOs get trained on their meanings to ensure clarity and alignment. If I'm told to feint, and my sister unit is told to assault, we both know exactly what that means and how we contribute to the team's overall success. Similarly, clearly defining Key Tasks in a business context prevents confusion and wasted effort. Continuing with our presentation example:

> **Sales Manager:** *"I need you to deliver a presentation to a potential client next month on our capabilities. The purpose is to convince them that we have the fastest technology available to meet their needs so we can close the deal by the end of the quarter.* ***Key to our success are three things: 1) understanding their current capabilities, 2) accurately forecasting their needs over the next few years, and 3) preparing for tough questions about MICRON Ltd., as their CEO seems to favor their technology."***
>
> **Sales Rep:** *"Got it. I'll contact their procurement officer and ask her to share what technology they've recently purchased. I'll also use our analytics to review growth projections and determine what will provide them ample future capacity. Finally, I'll get with Ted to better understand MICRON's tech and our biggest differentiators; he's the expert on their stuff. I'll have a draft by next Friday."*

By specifying Key Tasks, the Sales Manager provides enough direction for the report to exercise initiative without micromanagement. This balance avoids the frustration of needing to rework missing details later on while still empowering the team member.

End State – What does right look like in the end?

The End State paints a picture of what success looks like. It defines the outcome and sets the standard for evaluation. In the military, it might sound like, "Our End State is no sustained enemy penetration of our screen line, we maintain at least 80% combat power, and we are prepared to counterattack." This simple statement gives us a clear understanding of how we succeed together and informs decision-making. If the screen line is breached, plug the gap immediately or request support. If combat power drops below 80%, it may be time to organize a retreat to avoid further losses. If the mission goes well, don't get too comfortable and prepare for offensive operations. In business, it's also about envisioning a winning scenario. Finishing our presentation example:

Sales Manager: *"I need you to deliver a presentation to a potential client next month on our capabilities. The purpose is to convince them that we have the fastest technology available to meet their needs so we can close the deal by the end of the quarter. Key to our success are three things: 1) understanding their current capabilities, 2) accurately forecasting their needs over the next few years, and 3) preparing for tough questions about MICRON Ltd., as their CEO seems to favor their technology.* ***When the presentation is done, I want the client to feel 100% confident that we're their best option. They should have no doubts about our tech's superiority or our commitment to their growth. This is a family-owned company, so the presentation must feel informal and relationship-driven—not like a hard sell."***

Sales Rep: *"Got it. How about we take them out for a lunch meeting? I know the perfect place we can go. I'll reserve a private room that will allow for informal conversation and contribute to the outcome you are looking for. Also, I was originally thinking about creating a slide deck, but perhaps we should be more conversational. I'll have slides printed as a backup."*

Clarifying the End State enabled the Sales Representative to adapt their approach to align with the desired outcome. Initially, the assumption was that success meant delivering a formal presentation in the client's office. However, verbalizing the Sales Manager's vision of "what right looks like in the end" helped surface and refine these assumptions. As the conversation unfolds, both parties should further explore and clarify each other's expectations. For example, when does the Sales Manager want to review the draft slide deck? What meeting dates should they propose to the prospective client? Open dialogue helps refine assumptions, align expectations, and strengthen trust and accountability.

Finally, notice that at no point in communicating Commander's Intent did we specify *how* to accomplish the task. That decision is left entirely up to the individual. If someone is new to their role or the task at hand, additional guidance may be necessary to prevent confusion. Without this support, they might struggle, and their *Need for Direction* (discussed in Chapter 11) would overshadow their *Need for Autonomy*. However, in most cases, leaders should strive to provide less direction and more autonomy. If you consistently find yourself doing the opposite, it may be a sign that one of the disempowering mindsets mentioned earlier is holding you back.

Remember, the essence of Servant Leadership is prioritizing the needs of others over your own. This means setting aside your instinct to control and focusing on fulfilling others' *Need for Autonomy*. While this may be easier said than done, there are several practical strategies to help you "let go" more effectively.

Delegation Best Practices

Servant Leaders know that effective delegation and empowerment are essential for scaling leadership. Building trust is key to "letting go" and enabling others to thrive. Here are ten best practices to help you speed up the trust-building process and become a master delegator:

1. **Inventory Your Tasks Weekly** – Ask yourself, "What's ripe for delegating?" Then, assess the opportunity cost of handling it yourself. What could you get done that can't be delegated?
2. **Play to Strengths and Goals** – Know your team members' goals and career objectives. What tasks, if delegated, will allow for new learning that's aligned with their goals? Who's ready and eager to take on more?
3. **Redefine Yourself as a Facilitator** – Leaders often define their value as being problem-solvers. Instead, see yourself as the conduit in a system

of problem-solvers. Your value lies in organizing and directing resources, aligning tasks with talent strengths/needs, and maintaining the system.

4. **Start Small** – It's easier to delegate when the risk is low. Take baby steps. What tasks will allow for "failing forward" mistakes where learning is more important than perfect execution?
5. **Define Success** – Use *Commander's Intent* to help others prioritize, clarify assumptions, and visualize the desired outcome. Share how they will be evaluated.
6. **Plan Check-ins** – Periodic status updates will allow you to evaluate progress and course correct if things get off track. Yet, overdoing check-ins can lead to micromanaging. Balance autonomy with enough helpful support to enable success.
7. **Resist the Urge to Step In** – You may sometimes feel a strong urge to "fix things" or take over. Exercise restraint! Stepping in degrades trust in both directions. Avoid perfectionism and allow learning to occur. Assume the reigns only if intervention is critical.
8. **Believe in Them** – We all have a self-imposed ceiling on what we believe we can do. Often, it takes a new perspective for us to break through our inaccurate limitations. When a leader says we can do something, we start to believe we can. Express confidence to help others overcome self-doubt and unlock their potential.
9. **Open Lines of Communication** – Define expectations for how you will communicate. Encourage questions and feedback. Make it permissible for them to share with you what they need to be successful.
10. **Reward Performance & Give Credit** – Positively reinforce the behaviors you want to see more of. When someone successfully delivers on your intent, provide specific feedback on what they did well. Highlighting these successes encourages similar behaviors in future delegated tasks. Equally important, ensure that credit goes where it's due. If their contributions are mistaken for your work, it can demotivate them and make them less willing to take on delegated tasks in the future.

By implementing these practices, delegation becomes less daunting and more rewarding. Your team's growth and motivation will increase, freeing you to focus on higher-level strategic priorities. In time, you will start to experience the satisfaction of having the time to deal with those important but not urgent tasks that often fall by the wayside. Tapping into people's Need for Autonomy is a true win-win!

Fostering Autonomy Through Coaching

Developing an empowering mindset, employing Commander's Intent, and effectively delegating tasks are foundational strategies for addressing people's *Need for Autonomy*. Yet, the true game-changer for cultivating autonomy is the skill of coaching. Mastering coaching is a complex endeavor that takes years of practice, but the payoff is immense. Leaders who excel at coaching are highly sought after in today's fast-paced, dynamic workplace.

Consider the sporting world as a prime example. The best coaches are compensated at record levels because they consistently deliver results. Jim Harbaugh recently signed a five-year deal with the Los Angeles Chargers, reportedly earning an average annual salary of $16 million. Similarly, Erik Spoelstra secured the largest coaching contract in NBA history with an eight-year, $120 million extension with the Miami Heat. These deals highlight the immense value placed on leaders who know how to unlock potential and drive high performance. Talented players can only take a team so far; success ultimately requires the right coach to bring out their best.

Assessing coaching fit for a team can be challenging as cultures and dynamics differ significantly. One team may need a strong personality who challenges with high expectations. Another team might respond better to a light-hearted coach who empowers. Styles aside, what's most important is that a coach gets the most from their players and wins games. The same principle applies in business. Results are still the bottom line, but the methods leaders use to achieve those results have evolved. Modern leaders can no longer rely on directing and controlling execution. The pace and complexity of today's world demand a different approach. To scale their impact, leaders must create more leaders within their teams. This is why coaching has become one of the defining skills of exceptional leadership. Nothing develops future leaders faster than a coach who empowers others to unlock their potential.

How, then, do leaders become great coaches in today's workplace? It's a big question—one that could easily fill an entire book. While mastering coaching takes time, even the basics can deliver immediate results. I've trained thousands of managers on foundational coaching techniques, and it's remarkable how quickly they improve with just a little practice. Let's explore some of these key fundamentals.

When to Coach

The first step to effective coaching is knowing when it's the right approach. Coaching is about helping others learn and grow—it's not about teaching or advising. It's the opposite of telling someone what to do. Instead, coaching focuses on asking thoughtful, open-ended questions to draw out insights and solutions from the individual.

Coaching is most effective in these scenarios:

- **High Performers:** People who are ready for greater responsibility or new challenges benefit most from coaching.
- **Subject Matter Experts:** Coaching works well when the person you're coaching knows more about the problem than you do.
- **Ambiguous Problems:** When there isn't a clear-cut answer, coaching helps individuals explore possibilities and develop their own solutions.

However, coaching is not always the best choice:

- **For Beginners:** If someone is new to a task or skill, they likely need clear guidance and direction, not coaching.
- **For Black-and-White Issues:** Legal, compliance, or policy-related topics that require direct answers, not exploration.
- **Under Tight Deadlines:** In high-pressure or emergency situations, people need instructions, not coaching.
- **When You Already Know the Outcome:** Be transparent if you're set on a specific solution. Don't try to coach someone toward a pre-determined result; it can come across as manipulative.

Understanding when to coach—and when not to—is critical. Once you've identified the right moment, the next step is to focus on how to coach effectively. Servant Leaders excel at coaching by mastering three core skills: **Letting Go, Validating Data,** and **Guiding with the GROW Model.**

Letting Go

In Chapter 7, *The Need to Be Heard*, I emphasized how being fully present is the cornerstone of effective listening. Likewise, a calm and focused mind is crucial when starting a coaching conversation. But great coaching requires more than presence—it demands a shift in mindset. The goal isn't to provide answers but to facilitate learning. This can be challenging because most managers instinctively try to solve problems. If someone brings you a workplace challenge, isn't it your job to provide a solution? Not when you're coaching!

Servant Leaders resist the impulse to solve and instead adopt a mindset of curiosity. They allow themselves permission not to have all the answers or to be perfect. Letting go of the problem-solver identity is more difficult than it sounds. Many leaders define their value by their ability to fix issues—a mindset rooted in years of career reinforcement. Servant Leaders, however, understand that coaching isn't about solving; it's about facilitating. By stepping back, they empower their team to uncover creative and insightful solutions, often beyond what the leader could imagine.

Validating Data

Coaching requires a different level of listening that goes beyond surface facts to uncover the emotions driving the issue. Early in my coaching career, I focused on the factual aspects of problems, dismissing the "messy" emotional elements as distractions. I quickly learned that emotions are often the key to unlocking solutions.

For instance, a team member might struggle to influence a decision-maker, clash with a colleague, or feel unsure about their career path. In each case, emotions like frustration, anxiety, or doubt play a significant role. Start by acknowledging these feelings. Use reflective listening techniques like:

- "What I'm hearing is…"
- "It sounds like this experience was (frustrating, overwhelming, disappointing, etc.) for you."

This approach helps the person feel heard, enabling them to process emotions and transition to problem-solving with clarity.

Even more importantly, emotions provide valuable data. If someone feels dismissed by a decision-maker, focus on strategies to build confidence and optimism. If a colleague's domineering personality makes someone feel helpless, explore ways to feel more powerful and foster mutual respect. By identifying the emotions at play, you can guide the person toward solutions that address both the practical and emotional dimensions of the issue.

Guiding with the GROW Model

Many coaching frameworks exist, but the GROW model (Goal, Reality, Options, Will) is one of the most intuitive and effective. Here's how it works:

Goal – What do you want?

Reality – What's the current situation?

Options – What can you try?

Will – What will you do next?

Although the model appears linear, GROW conversations rarely unfold step by step. You might revisit earlier stages or jump ahead as new insights emerge. This flexibility allows the conversation to uncover root issues and actionable goals organically.

Here's an example of a coaching conversation using the GROW model:

Coachee: *"Do you have a minute? I'd like your advice on something."*

Don't fall for the advice trap. Get present and be curious.

Coach: *"Sure thing. I have about 10 minutes before my next meeting. What's on your mind?"*

Coachee: *"One of my team leaders, who's usually a high performer, seems distracted lately."*

You can't possibly be an expert on why their team leader is distracted, so it's the perfect time to coach.

Coach: *"Tell me more. How could I be helpful to you in this situation?"*
This begins the **G**oal step: identifying the broader issue and setting a goal for the conversation..

Coachee: *"I want to figure out what's distracting him and how to get him back on track."*
Coach: *"What signs are you seeing that indicate he's distracted? How is this impacting his performance?"*
This moves into the **R**eality step, exploring the current situation to build a clear picture. Good coaches don't spend too much time here. The aim is to gain additional context and build creative tension between the current state and the desired future state.

Coachee: *"He's been skipping meetings and missing details in his reports. This is unusual for him."*
Coach: *"What do you think might be going on? What assumptions are you making? What have you tried so far?"*
A good coach helps their coachee distinguish between facts and assumptions. For example, the team leader in question may not be distracted but more annoyed or withdrawn. Help them ground their observations in facts.

Coachee: *"I spoke to him briefly, but he just said he has some personal stuff going on. I didn't press him. I'm not sure what else to do."*
Coach: *"What about the timing or setting of your conversation might have affected his response? How could you create a more comfortable space for him to open up?"*
Now, we're in the **O**ptions stage, where the coach helps brainstorm ideas by asking smart and powerful questions. You'll likely feel a strong urge to prescribe

solutions during this stage. Bite your lip and instead use your intuition to form a question. The best questions for opening up possibilities always start with "What" or "How." For example, instead of saying, "Have you thought about doing your next meeting over a coffee instead of in the office?" Say, "How could you create a more comfortable space for him to open up?" The idea is that when they produce an option (rather than you), they have more ownership and intrinsic motivation to act on it.

Coachee: *"I approached him at the end of the day, and I could tell he wanted to wrap up his work and get home. It probably wasn't the best timing. It was also in the hallway where others might have heard our conversation. I should get him out of the office to a more comfortable setting."*

Coach: *"That sounds like a good idea... What's your plan, and when will you try to have the conversation?*

Now we're in the **W**ill stage, where the coach helps the coachee solidify their next steps and commit to action.

Coachee: *"I'll invite him to lunch next Monday and share my own story about dealing with personal challenges. My goal is to build trust and see how I can help him succeed."*

Coach: *"Excellent. I'll follow up with you afterward to see how it went."*

The 80/20 Rule for Coaching

In an effective coaching conversation, the coachee should do 80% of the talking, with the coach asking questions for the remaining 20%. If the balance shifts, it's likely because the coach is trying too hard to solve the problem. Servant Leaders trust their team's ability to find their own solutions, enabling them to build confidence and autonomy.

If you are hesitant about this process, try it out. It can initially feel awkward as you refrain from providing answers and fumble to identify good questions. However, one of the best moments in coaching is when your coachee offers a solution you would never have thought of. It's a great feeling to see their own brilliance manifest and know you played a small part in facilitating that wisdom to unfold.

Serving the Need for Autonomy

Humans are hardwired to resist control and crave autonomy. Leaders who embrace this reality build trust, empower their teams, and foster greater engagement. By mastering tools like Commander's Intent, delegation, and coaching, Servant Leaders unlock their team's potential and create the conditions for scalable, effective leadership. Empowered teams aren't just a benefit—they're a necessity in today's complex and fast-paced world.

Self-Assess

How likely is your team to say you micro-manage their work?

1-----------2------------3------------4------------5------------6------------7

Honestly, they might say I get too involved

I have a reputation for empowering others

How often do you explain "the why" behind a task request

1-----------2------------3------------4------------5------------6------------7

It's rarely my priority

I always connect tasks to a relevant purpose

How many of the ten delegation best practices are you doing?

1-----------2------------3------------4------------5------------6------------7

Only one or two of them, delegation is difficult for me

I'm already doing nine or ten of these best practices well

How effectively do you coach people to find their own solutions?

1-----------2------------3------------4------------5------------6------------7

I prefer to provide advice and to mentor instead

I routinely ask smart questions and facilitate ideas

Scoring:

24-28 = Congrats! Your team likely feels empowered and motivated

13-23 = People may feel empowered at times, but there are times when their need for autonomy goes unfulfilled

4-12 = Autonomy may be an underserved need on your team

Reflect

What mindsets impede you from delegating and empowering others? When are they most likely to show up for you?

Who on your team is ready for more? What steps will you take to delegate more to your team? How will these steps allow you to elevate your thinking, and what might you be able to accomplish?

What's the biggest obstacle to you being a good coach?

a. Getting fully present and listening for emotional data
b. Not trying to personally solve the problem for them
c. Asking smart and powerful questions that open up ideas

Recap

- Autonomy fuels motivation, ownership, and innovation. When people feel trusted to make decisions, they become more engaged, confident, and fulfilled.
- Common disempowering mindsets—like believing "they'll do it wrong" or "I can't afford mistakes"—keep leaders stuck in control rather than building scalable leadership through others.
- Use Commander's Intent as a tool for greater empowerment:
  - Purpose: Explain why the work matters to inspire initiative and commitment.
  - Key Tasks: Outline what must happen without over-prescribing how it's done.
  - End State: Define what success looks like so teams can self-adjust and align outcomes.
- Delegate to foster trust: Identify tasks to delegate weekly, aligning them with team members' strengths and goals, and start small to allow for learning.
- Coaching accelerates growth: Shift from problem-solver to facilitator, use the GROW model, and guide high performers to uncover their own solutions.

9

THE NEED TO BE CHALLENGED

Most people assume fighting in a war is one of the most terrifying experiences imaginable. While many veterans would agree that combat is chaotic and the possibility of injury or death is unsettling, there's a surprising twist to this narrative. For me, the most nerve-wracking moments as an Officer weren't during my 15-month deployment to Iraq—they happened back in Garrison during periods of extended downtime.

You might be wondering, "How does that make sense?" Let me explain. Soldiers spend most of their time training to be confident and ready for combat. While the conditions of a combat deployment can be grueling, soldiers often thrive when their skills are put to the test. Every day demands their best because mistakes can be costly—sometimes fatally so.

In contrast, Garrison life often involves mundane tasks like routine maintenance and administrative work. For the Cavalry units I served with, days in Garrison quickly became repetitive, leading to restlessness. After a few weeks of recovery operations, soldiers were itching to return to the field for more training.

Why was I apprehensive about these downtimes? Because a bored soldier is looking for trouble. They can party hard, drink too much, oversleep, get in fights, gamble, buy cars they can't afford at 32% interest, or spontaneously marry strippers (not kidding). When you are a young, unchallenged soldier, engaging in risky behavior breaks the monotony. As a Troop Commander, I was often called back to Post to deal with "situations." My hope each time was that no one had been injured or committed a serious offense, like a DUI. Did this behavior also occur when we were in the field or deployed? Of course not! My soldiers were always laser-focused on the mission and acted with professionalism.

Over time, I realized soldiers must be challenged daily, regardless of the environment. If the day required tedious vehicle maintenance in the motor pool, we'd plan a five-mile run during morning PT to balance it out. If we scheduled a session of weapons cleaning, we'd also incorporate crew-level training in simulators. The idea was simple: a physically and mentally tired soldier is less likely to seek additional stimulation in unproductive ways. At the end of such days, they'd typically want nothing more than a good night's sleep to recharge for the next day's challenges.

While this example is from a military setting, the principle applies to workplaces everywhere. Without appropriate challenges, people disengage. Boredom, restlessness, irritability, and even stagnation creep in. Without growth, mediocrity becomes the norm, and over time, decline may follow.

When employees feel unchallenged, they often seek new opportunities elsewhere. Best-selling author Daniel Pink highlights this phenomenon in his book *Drive*, describing Mastery as a key motivator. His research shows that people are intrinsically driven to improve their skills because continuous growth feels good—it fosters a sense of control over one's environment.[13] I refer to this concept as *The Need for Challenge* because it makes the idea more actionable for leaders. While you can't control a team member's level of mastery, you can ensure they're adequately challenged.

Using the Challenge and Support Levers

As a leader, you have two essential levers to motivate and grow your team: the **challenge lever** and the **support lever**. The challenge lever increases stress and pushes individuals to expand their capabilities. The support lever, on the other hand, reduces stress, ensuring people don't become overwhelmed or burned out. The key is to balance these levers and keep your team members in the "Zone of Motivation."

The challenge lever should be increased to the point where team members feel discomfort but not to the point of breaking them. Too little challenge results in superficial motivation, requiring constant rechallenging. Too much challenge, however, risks demoralizing or exhausting them. Servant Leaders understand the importance of monitoring progress and emotions to maintain this balance. Perhaps you observe someone struggling in a new role and getting frustrated. You might choose to maintain the same level of challenge but increase your support. Or you could pull back on the challenge entirely and go all-in on support until they regain their confidence. Effective leaders continuously adjust these levers to ensure their people remain engaged, motivated, and growing.

Maintaining The Zone of Motivation

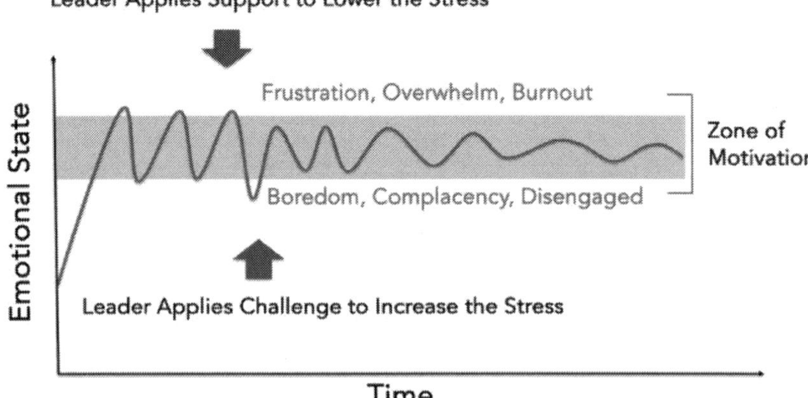

We know motivation thrives when people are learning, mastering skills, and increasing competency. Yet, leaders sometimes mistakenly assume their team members are satisfied where they are. Take, for example, a high-performing engineer who declines a management position, citing a preference for technical work over people leadership. It's easy to interpret this as a lack of interest in further challenges, but that would be a mistake. While they may not want to manage others, this doesn't mean they're content to stagnate in their current role.

In such cases, the leader must find alternative ways to challenge them. Assigning a difficult project or asking them to mentor junior engineers could reignite their engagement and motivation. Without such opportunities, even the most talented individuals can become disengaged and eventually leave for an environment that offers the challenges they crave. Servant Leaders care deeply about keeping their team members sharp and engaged. They regularly assess motivation levels and make the necessary adjustments to ensure their people are appropriately challenged.

How to Inspire with Challenge

The word *challenge* can sometimes carry negative connotations. For instance, someone described as "challenging to work with" might be viewed as difficult or uncooperative. Similarly, if someone is "facing challenges," it's usually a polite way of saying they're struggling or underperforming. And think about the discomfort of having your idea challenged by a peer in a team meeting—being put on the spot can feel downright uncomfortable.

But challenges can also be incredibly positive. A good challenge makes life interesting, fuels personal growth, and provides a sense of purpose. Striving for something meaningful and overcoming obstacles delivers profound satisfaction. When a leader appropriately challenges their team, it can be deeply inspiring. So, how does a leader inspire through challenge? There are three critical components: **setting high expectations, providing feedback, and maintaining accountability**.

Setting High Expectations

At first glance, setting expectations seems straightforward. After all, people need to know what's expected of them to meet those expectations. Yet, a global Gallup survey reveals that only about half of employees strongly agree that they understand what's expected of them at work.[14] Why is this disconnect so prevalent?

One reason is that many leaders struggle to communicate expectations clearly because they haven't fully defined them for themselves. Setting expectations requires intentionality. Leaders must define performance goals, connect individual roles to company objectives, and articulate how success will be measured.

In addition to performance metrics, leaders should communicate the behaviors they value and expect. For example:

- Do you prioritize personal initiative and competitive spirit or collaboration and teamwork?
- What types of decisions should your team members make independently?
- How frequently do you want updates, and in what level of detail?
- How should sensitive or bad news be communicated?
- How will you handle feedback—both giving and receiving?

Explicitly sharing these expectations helps eliminate ambiguity and provides a roadmap for success.

Another reason leaders fail to set expectations is discomfort. Setting high expectations should push people to grow beyond their current abilities. This means people can't relax and be satisfied with the status quo. They'll have to work hard and experience growing pains that most people prefer to avoid. Even high achievers might prefer a low bar that allows them to coast to an "exceeds expectations" rating on their annual review. However, allowing this mindset prevents individuals from reaching their full potential.

Some leaders shy away from setting high expectations out of fear of demotivating their teams. They may worry that pushing too hard will lead to dissatisfaction or disloyalty. However, Servant Leaders understand that holding people to high standards isn't about being demanding for the sake of it—it's about empowering them to achieve their best. Failing to challenge your team does them a disservice. Growth doesn't happen in a comfort zone.

A SMART framework—**Specific, Measurable, Achievable, Relevant, Time-bound**—is an excellent tool when setting high-performance goals. Let's look at an example for a sales professional:.

- **Specific:** Increase sales productivity by 15% in the next quarter.
- **Measurable:** Achieve this by booking 10 meetings weekly, making 5 phone calls daily, and prospecting to 100 people monthly.
- **Achievable:** This goal is realistic because a 15% increase is challenging but manageable, especially with new products providing a competitive edge.
- **Relevant:** The company's goal is to increase revenue by $200M next quarter, and a 15% increase in personal productivity will make the salesperson a significant contributor.
- **Time-bound:** There is one quarter for preparation and one quarter for execution, allowing six months to achieve the goal.

Setting SMART Goals

This framework ensures clarity and alignment. Success (or lack thereof) is evident at the end of the quarter. You might even start with a stretch goal—say, a 25% increase—and engage in a dialogue to determine what's realistic yet challenging. Negotiating the goal ensures buy-in. Once the goal is set, express confidence in your team member's ability to succeed, pledge your support, and provide the necessary resources.

Finally, some leaders avoid setting high expectations because it holds them accountable too. Once you establish expectations, you can't just hope things go according to plan—you must follow up. That means providing consistent support, coaching, training, and mentoring. It also requires holding people accountable when they fall short. Let's be honest: This adds to an already overburdened leader's workload. It's tempting to set lower expectations to save time and avoid the extra pressure.

But Servant Leaders know this is self-serving behavior, and they resist the urge to take the easy way out. Avoiding high expectations to make your job easier is a disservice to your team—and, ultimately, your organization. Properly setting and supporting high expectations is how leaders inspire growth and foster success.

Increasing Performance through Feedback

Providing constructive feedback is one of the most powerful ways a leader can meet an individual's *Need for Challenge*. Yet, many leaders either fail to deliver feedback effectively or avoid it altogether. Consider these statistics from recent large-scale surveys conducted by Gallup, AllVoices, and Office Vibe[15]:

- 96% of employees say regular feedback is beneficial.
- 75% report not receiving feedback frequently enough to improve their performance.
- 64% believe the quality of the feedback they receive could be improved.
- Only 10% of employees feel engaged after receiving negative feedback.

These numbers are telling. Employees overwhelmingly want more feedback—specifically actionable, constructive feedback to improve their performance. Yet, when they do receive feedback, it's often not helpful and can even reduce engagement. This gap is a significant problem because feedback is one of the most effective tools leaders have to unlock potential and drive results. So why is feedback lacking in today's workplace?

The reasons vary. Sometimes, it's due to a lack of proper feedback systems or insufficient prioritization. However, the most common reason is fear. Leaders often hesitate to give feedback, worrying:

- "What if I don't say it perfectly?"
- "What if my feedback is wrong?"
- "What if they get upset?"
- "I have to work with this person every day."
- "I want to maintain a good relationship with my team."
- "What if they perceive my feedback as biased?"

Notice a pattern? These concerns revolve around the leader's own fears and discomfort—not the needs of the person receiving feedback. Servant Leaders recognize when their fears are holding them back and choose to act courageously. They understand that providing feedback is essential to their role. If it doesn't come from them, where will it come from? Servant Leaders take ownership of their responsibility to help others improve and reach their potential.

But why is feedback often delivered so poorly? You've likely heard the saying, "Feedback is a gift," yet it doesn't always feel that way. Many of us have experienced clumsy feedback sessions with a boss. The feedback is either too harsh, triggering defensiveness, or vague, leaving us confused. It lacks actionable details or examples, and instead of feeling grateful for receiving helpful guidance, we walk away upset or frustrated.

Fortunately, there are simple ways to avoid these outcomes. Over the past decade, I've worked extensively with managers on delivering feedback that reduces defensiveness and inspires action. Based on this experience, here are five best practices for providing constructive feedback.

Constructive Feedback: A Servant Leader's Approach

1. **Mindset Awareness**

   Before providing feedback, check your mindset. Are you trying to "fix" them, or are you genuinely trying to serve them? Viewing someone as a "problem to solve" communicates judgment, which often triggers defensiveness. No one likes feeling like they're being "fixed!" On the other hand, if your intention is rooted in care and a desire to help them improve, they'll be far more open to what you have to say. When you embody a servant's mindset, your language, tone, and posture naturally convey respect and support, making it easier for the recipient to receive your feedback.

2. **Gain Buy-In**

   Start with a simple question: "May I give you some feedback?" While it seems minor, this step is crucial. It ensures the other person is ready and willing to hear your input. Perhaps they're having a tough day or aren't in the right frame of mind. Asking permission shows respect, empowers them to say yes, and creates a collaborative tone for the conversation.

3. **Use the SBI Framework**

   The SBI model—*Situation, Behavior, Impact*—is an invaluable tool for structuring your feedback effectively:

   - **Situation:** Describe the specific context where the behavior occurred.

- **Behavior:** Focus on observable actions or behaviors, avoiding personal judgments.
- **Impact:** Explain how their behavior affected others, the team, or the organization.

Example:

(S) ituation – *"During your presentation today to the team…."*

(B) ehavior – *"When you reached slide five, Bill tried asking a question, and you asked him to please hold questions until the end as there was a lot to cover."*

(I) mpact – *"I noticed some people tune out almost immediately and start checking their phones. No one brought up questions at the end. I'm concerned people lost interest, and you missed potentially valuable input. You worked hard on this presentation, and your ideas deserve to be heard. I also know that enhancing your communication skills is a personal goal for you to become more promotable. How can we better integrate questions into your next presentation?"*

4. **Get Curious and Create Space**
   After delivering feedback, transition into listening mode. Ask for their perspective: "How did you view the situation?" or "What are your thoughts on what I shared?" This creates a dialogue and shows you value their input. Be prepared for emotional responses—some people process feedback differently. Acknowledge their feelings, empathize, and keep the conversation focused on growth. If the discussion starts to veer off-topic, gently guide it back to their performance.

5. **Practice, Practice, Practice**
   The more you practice giving feedback, the better you'll become. Many leaders struggle with finding the right words to convey their intentions effectively. Don't leave feedback conversations to chance—rehearse them. Write down what you want to say and then practice with a trusted colleague or mentor. Ask them for feedback on your delivery. Was it clear and actionable? Did you trigger any feelings of defensiveness? How was your body language? Rehearsing ensures you approach the real conversation with confidence and clarity.

When done well, feedback is transformational. It strengthens relationships, drives performance, and empowers people to grow. By following these best practices, you can deliver feedback in a way that feels like the gift it's meant to be—one that inspires growth, trust, and mutual respect.

Maintaining Accountability to Inspire

When you hear the word "accountability," what comes to mind? For many, it conjures images of tough conversations about missed expectations—"holding people accountable," often in a stern and unmotivating way. That perspective feels negative, doesn't it? It doesn't have to be that way. When done right, accountability shows you care about the individual and are committed to excellence. A leader who cares deeply and upholds high standards earns respect, and respect inspires.

We all aspire to be the best version of ourselves, yet often, we get in our own way. Think about hiring a personal trainer at the gym. Sure, their fitness expertise is valuable, but their real gift is keeping us focused and committed to our goals. On days we'd rather skip the gym, the knowledge that our trainer is waiting gets us moving. After the workout, we feel proud of our effort, and the results in the mirror remind us why it was worth it. This is the power of accountability—it helps us achieve what we might not accomplish alone.

The Leader's Role in Accountability

When leaders set high expectations, they must recognize that meeting them won't always be smooth sailing. There will be highs and lows. A Servant Leader keeps people in the "Zone of Motivation" by applying the right balance of challenge and support. When people face frustration, overwhelm, or burnout, the leader provides empathy and assistance. Strong empathy is essential for compassionate and useful action. Servant Leaders identify where support is most needed by stepping into their team members' shoes and "feeling" their pain points.

However, empathy has its limits. Excessive support without sufficient challenge can sometimes enable excuses for unmet expectations. This is where the Servant Leader must make the difficult choice to apply "tough love." Maintaining a high standard—and sometimes adding discipline to reinforce it—can feel uncomfortable for everyone involved. But true service means holding people to their potential, even when it's hard. Lowering the bar might seem like the easier option in the moment, but if you genuinely believe in someone's ability to meet high expectations, stand firm and continue to challenge them. Sometimes, maintaining pressure is exactly what they need to unlock better performance and achieve their best.

The Power of Belief

One of the most inspiring ways to maintain accountability is by voicing your belief in others. Each of us carries self-limiting beliefs shaped by our past successes and failures. These beliefs often act as invisible ceilings, keeping us from pushing beyond our comfort zones—unless someone helps us break through.

A Servant Leader recognizes this and leverages the power of belief. When team members struggle to meet a high standard, remind them of their capability. Point to past successes, express unwavering confidence, and affirm their potential. This isn't just a motivational tactic; it actively shifts how people see themselves.

When a leader I admire tells me they believe I can succeed—even when I doubt myself—it changes my mindset. I begin to think, "Maybe they're right. Maybe I *can* do this." This recalibration of self-belief is transformative. As a leader, I experienced many moments where I wasn't sure someone could rise to a challenge, yet I chose to express confidence in them anyway. Time and time again, they have surprised me by exceeding expectations. Had I voiced my doubts, they might never have reached their potential. Your people will rise or fall to the level of your expectations.

Serving the Need for Challenge

The *Need for Challenge* requires leaders to lean into discomfort. Setting high expectations, delivering constructive feedback, and maintaining accountability can feel edgy, even confrontational. But these are acts of service. We all need challenges to grow, and as a leader, your role is to push people toward their best selves. Be the leader who inspires others to rise to their potential. Your team may not appreciate being challenged immediately, but over time, they'll respect the gift you gave them and respect you for it.

Self-Assess

How well do you keep your people in the "zone of motivation"?

1----------2-----------3-----------4-----------5-----------6-----------7

I struggle with knowing how much challenge or support to offer

I read people well and apply appropriate support and challenge

How well do you communicate high expectations?

1----------2-----------3-----------4-----------5-----------6-----------7

I don't like pushing people too hard

I challenge people to meet their full potential

How often do you give constructive feedback?

1----------2-----------3-----------4-----------5-----------6-----------7

I rarely give people constructive feedback

I consistently give specific, actionable, and timely constructive feedback

How well do you maintain accountability to expectations?

1----------2-----------3-----------4-----------5-----------6-----------7

I'm uncomfortable with holding others accountable

I can inspirationally maintain accountability

Scoring:

24-28 = Congrats! You are likely challenging people in a healthy way and bringing out their full potential

13-23 = While your team may feel moderately challenged, there is likely latent potential on your team going untapped

4-12 = Challenge may be an underserved need on your team

Reflect

What signs indicate that someone needs to be challenged more? What behaviors suggest it's time to reduce their level of challenge and provide additional support?

How do you set high expectations that elevate performance without being unrealistic and demotivating the team?

How can you improve the way you deliver constructive feedback? Should you focus on serving rather than fixing? Would using the SBI model be helpful? Can you be more consistent or timely?

How do you typically maintain accountability as a leader? What's your style, and how effective is it?

Recap

- Without challenges, boredom and disengagement set in, leading to decreased motivation, mediocrity, and poor performance.
- Leaders must balance the challenge and support levers to keep employees in the "Zone of Motivation."
- Leaders should set high expectations, offer constructive feedback, and maintain accountability to inspire growth.
- Use the SBI model (Situation, Behavior, Impact) to give constructive feedback that is respectful and focused on improvement.
- Accountability is a sign of care. Leaders should hold their teams to high standards with empathy, offering support when needed, but also applying "tough love" when necessary to ensure growth.
- Expressing belief in team members, even when they struggle, can help them surpass their self-limiting beliefs and reach their full potential.
- Challenging others is uncomfortable, but it is an act of service. Leaders must push their people to achieve their best, knowing that their challenge is a gift that will lead to long-term growth and respect.

10

THE NEED FOR RECOGNITION

As a leader, recognizing high performers on your team is part of your responsibility. While it may not be explicitly outlined in a job description, it's an unsaid expectation that comes with the role. We assume leaders understand the value of recognition and trust they'll do it naturally. However, if you reflect on your career, you've likely encountered leaders who excelled at recognizing performance and others who failed miserably. Why the inconsistency? Recognizing others isn't exactly a complex skill. At its core, it involves noticing actions and acknowledging those who meet or exceed expectations. Simple, right? Apparently not.

Recent studies consistently reveal that more recognition is needed in the workplace. A 2023 Quantum Workplace study found that **only 35% of employees receive recognition monthly or weekly**, yet **half of all employees want more acknowledgment for their work.**[16] A 2022 Gallup study showed that **67% of leaders and 61% of managers provide recognition several times a week**, but **40% of employees still report being recognized only a few times a year or less.**[17]

The implications of these gaps are significant. When employees feel undervalued, they're more likely to disengage, seek validation elsewhere, or quietly quit—putting in the bare minimum to avoid being fired. Leaders can no longer assume they're giving enough recognition. Instead, the assumption should be that they're not doing enough.

So why isn't recognition happening as much as it should? Why are some leaders better at it than others?

Mindset Malfunctions

After years of working with managers, I've observed recurring reasons why recognition falls short. One of my favorite questions to ask leaders in training programs is: **"How often are you noticing the good around you and providing positive feedback?"**

The responses are telling. Many pause, then reluctantly admit, "Yeah, I need to do that more often." Others defend their approach with, "I give feedback, but I don't want to overdo it because it might lose its value." The idea that recognition loses its impact if given too often is a misconception—a mindset malfunction. Think about it: Have you ever wished someone appreciated your work less? Have you ever thought, "I really wish my boss would stop noticing how well I'm doing"? Probably not.

> **"The deepest principle of Human Nature is the craving to be appreciated."**
>
> *- William James, American philosopher and psychologist*

The truth is, we all want to feel valued—every day. You may think, "This may be true for others, but not for me." Even if you believe you personally don't need constant praise, don't project that onto others. It's a blind spot many leaders have: "I don't need recognition, so my team probably doesn't either." But the reality is that most people thrive on acknowledgment. And if you received more praise, you probably wouldn't mind it either.

Another mindset malfunction is the belief that recognition isn't necessary because people are "just doing their job that we pay them for." Yes, they're compensated for their work, but that doesn't mean their efforts should go unappreciated. Servant Leaders make it a point to acknowledge even the routine or "trivial" tasks that might seem insignificant to others. These often-overlooked contributions become glaringly important when they're missed—and that's when everyone realizes the true value of those performing them.

Leaders also overlook opportunities to recognize behaviors not directly related to organizational results. For instance, a team member who brings in a birthday cake and leads a cheerful celebration fosters a positive culture. Or the teammate who consistently shows up with an optimistic energy, lifting the entire team's morale. These contributions, while intangible, are worthy of praise, gratitude, and appreciation—or, as I like to call it, PGA.

Cleaning Up the Mindset

When a rifle fails to fire in the Army, it's called a malfunction. The solution is often simple: clean and lubricate the weapon. Similarly, Servant Leaders must "clean up" their thinking to address mindset malfunctions about recognition. The problem is that leaders are natural problem-solvers. They're constantly scanning for what's broken or inefficient and how to fix it. This focus on what's wrong often blinds them to what's right.

To overcome this, leaders must deliberately develop the habit of "looking for the good." Start noticing small contributions alongside big accomplishments. Praise someone not only when they exceed expectations but also for the little things that make a positive impact. When you regularly practice PGA, you unlock the power of recognition. By paying attention to the good happening around you and consistently acknowledging it, you inspire your team and create a culture where people feel valued every day.

The Golden Rule of Recognition

One of the quickest ways to lose influence as a leader is to take credit for something you didn't do. It seems basic, almost too obvious to mention, yet it happens far too often. In conducting 360-degree feedback interviews for executives, I've repeatedly heard stories of leaders who claim credit for others' ideas, attribute team successes to their own efforts, or imply they were solely responsible for achievements they had little to do with. These behaviors erode trust almost instantly, and rebuilding that trust is incredibly difficult.

When leaders take credit for their team's accomplishments, team members eventually stop sharing ideas directly with them. Sometimes, leaders don't blatantly steal credit but don't share it when it's due. This usually occurs in hyper-competitive environments where promotions are hard to come by. The damage is the same either way. Don't be that kind of leader!

The Golden Rule of Recognition is simple: immediately pass on any credit you receive to those who deserve it. Not tomorrow, not during your next team meeting—right now. A Servant Leader graciously accepts praise on behalf of the team and promptly redirects the credit to those responsible. Whether or not the team members are present, acknowledge their contributions. If the praise comes via email, reply by cc'ing the relevant team members and highlighting their specific actions. If meeting with more senior leaders and you receive praise, respond graciously and use the opportunity to give visibility to your team's work.

> **"It's been my experience that people that gain trust, loyalty, excitement, and energy fast are the ones who pass credit on to the people who have really done the work. A leader does not need credit...He's getting more than he deserves anyway."**
>
> *- Robert Townsend, Author of "Up the Organization"*

Get in the habit of promoting your team instead of yourself. As the leader, others already know you're responsible for the team's results. But would you rather they think, "This leader is indispensable because of their own efforts," or "This leader inspires, empowers, and develops talent to deliver exceptional results?" Remember, as discussed in *Chapter 4: Be Redundant to Get Promoted*, your success depends on making your team's success the focus. Elevating your team isn't just the right thing to do—it's also the smart thing for your career.

Recognition Best Practice – Knowing Praise Preferences

While recognizing others may seem straightforward, some nuances separate good leaders from great ones. One of the most important things is understanding how each team member likes to be recognized. When managing a new team, this should be one of the first conversations during your initial one-on-one meetings. Share that you want to recognize your team as much as possible and would like to know how they like to receive praise. Publicly or privately? Verbally or in writing? Are there specific rewards or incentives they value most?"

Avoid projecting your own preferences onto your team. For example, as an extroverted leader, you might enjoy public recognition and assume others will, too. But imagine pulling Kathy in front of the team to highlight her recent achievement, only to realize she's mortified. She's an introvert who would've appreciated a quiet thank-you email instead. Tailoring recognition to individual preferences ensures it lands as intended.

Be mindful of the team member who says, "I don't need or want recognition." This could be them being humble, or it could also signal discomfort with being acknowledged. They may fear standing out, being perceived as a "kiss ass," or drawing unwanted attention. Thoughtful, consistent recognition delivered according to their preferences can help overcome this. When done right, even the most reluctant individuals come to appreciate being valued.

Remember, feeling appreciated is a fundamental human need. If someone insists they don't want recognition, don't take it at face value. Over time, neglecting to acknowledge their contributions could leave them feeling undervalued. Approach this with care, and you'll foster a culture where everyone feels seen and appreciated.

Recognition Best Practice - The 3/1 Ratio

An essential best practice for recognition is maintaining the right balance between positive and constructive feedback. Research across various organizations has revealed an optimal ratio for building trust: three instances of positive feedback for every one piece of constructive feedback.[18] This means that for every "here's where you need to improve" conversation, a leader should deliver three "well done" or "great job" acknowledgments. Ideally, positive feedback should precede any constructive feedback conversations.

I call this investing coins in the credibility bank. Employees are far more receptive to constructive feedback when it comes from a leader who has consistently recognized their achievements. Each acknowledgment of positive performance builds credibility, giving leaders the capital to have more challenging conversations when necessary.

Why the 3/1 Ratio Works

Not all feedback carries the same weight. Our brains are naturally wired to focus on potential threats, making constructive feedback or criticism stick with us longer. When a leader points out areas for improvement, our minds can spiral. Does my boss think less of me? Will this hurt my chances for a promotion? Maybe I should start looking for a new job! This heightened emotional response makes constructive feedback incredibly "sticky." In contrast, positive feedback feels good for a hot minute but fades quickly—it's like Teflon, sliding off our minds without leaving much impact.

If a 3/1 ratio sounds excessive, consider this: it's recommended for ideal environments where trust is already established. For average environments, the ratio jumps to 5/1. In toxic environments where distrust and negativity dominate, the ideal ratio skyrockets to 9/1. To determine the appropriate ratio for your team, ask yourself:

- Is management perceived as supportive or untrustworthy?
- How transparent is the culture with sharing information?
- Do people tend to collaborate or compete?
- How are mistakes handled—are they seen as learning opportunities or grounds for blame?

In less trusting environments, you may need to invest even more heavily in recognizing good performance before addressing areas for improvement.

On a side note, what do you think is the proper ratio of positive to constructive feedback for a healthy marriage? When I ask this question in my training programs, many people jokingly yell out, "1000/1!" While that may seem about right, the correct answer is 5/1. That means five "Thanks for all you do" and "I love you" comments for every "I need you to wash the dishes more often" comment![19]

A Note on the Feedback Sandwich

Some leaders mistakenly think the 3/1 ratio must be delivered within a single conversation—this is where the infamous "feedback sandwich" comes into play. It typically sounds like this:

> *"You're doing great at [positive feedback], but you need to improve at [constructive feedback]. That said, overall, I'm happy with your performance [positive feedback]."*

While the intention is to soften the blow, this approach can confuse the recipient. Are they doing well, or are they not?

Instead, separate your feedback. Recognize good performance in its own conversation. Offer praise when it's due. Acknowledge effort with gratitude. Then, when it's time to address areas for improvement, have that discussion independently. Your prior recognition builds the credibility needed for clearer, more productive dialogue during constructive feedback.

Recognition Best Practice – Language Matters

Does a simple "thank you" resonate as profoundly as "I really appreciate you for doing that"? What about a generic "Good job on the presentation" versus "I thought your presentation was brilliant"? In both cases, the latter options carry more weight and feel more meaningful. While it might seem trivial, language matters, and leaders must choose their words thoughtfully, especially when offering Praise, Gratitude, and Appreciation (PGA).

A Servant Leader understands that recognition, when done correctly, is one of the most powerful motivators available. A sincere expression of gratitude can fuel a team member's motivation for weeks—but for it to have this effect, it must be delivered with care. The significance of the words should match the level of the team member's actions.

Crafting Impactful Recognition

In my experience working with leaders who want to improve their recognition skills, one common challenge is finding the right words and tone. To address this, I created a language hierarchy to guide leaders in delivering meaningful recognition.

PGA (Praise, Gratitude, and Appreciation) Guide

Use this guide to reinforce positive behaviors, build morale, and strengthen team cohesion.

4. Deep Personal Recognition (Profound Impact)
- You are an invaluable part of this team, and I deeply appreciate everything you do.
- Your work has left a lasting impact, and I want to personally thank you for that.
- The way you handled [situation] was remarkable. You truly embody our values.
- You're a game-changer, and we're lucky to have you.

3. High-Impact Appreciation (Major Contributions)
- You've set a new benchmark for excellence!
- Your work has made a significant impact on [specific project/team].
- I'm consistently impressed by your ability to [specific skill or contribution].
- We couldn't have achieved this without you.
- Your leadership in this situation was truly inspiring.

2. Performance Recognition (Above-Average Effort)
- That was excellent work! You went above and beyond.
- Your attention to detail really made a difference.
- I'm grateful for your dedication and extra effort.
- Your hard work on [specific task] was outstanding!
- You really stepped up and delivered when we needed it.

1. Everyday Acknowledgment (Frequent, Light Praise)
- Thanks for your effort on this!
- Nice job on that task!
- I appreciate your help.
- Well done! Keep it up.
- That was a solid contribution.

1. **Use Daily – Everyday Acknowledgment**
   At the base of the chart, you'll find light, everyday praise—simple phrases like "Thanks for your effort" or "Nice job on that task." These should be used often and freely. Regular recognition of small wins helps build morale, maintain momentum, and create a culture of appreciation.
2. **Above-Average Effort – Performance Recognition**
   As you move up the chart, the language carries more weight. This level is for recognizing when someone goes beyond expectations. It's about calling out extra effort and solid performance with phrases like "You really stepped up" or "That was excellent work!" Use this when contributions stand out from the norm.
3. **Major Contributions – High-Impact Appreciation**
   Higher still, the appreciation becomes more significant. This level is for major wins, leadership moments, or impactful contributions. Comments like "You've set a new benchmark" or "We couldn't have done this without you" show that their work made a real difference. Use this language selectively to reinforce key moments of success.
4. **Use Sparingly – Deep Personal Recognition**
   At the very top sits the most powerful, personal recognition. This language carries profound emotional weight and should be used only for exceptional, lasting impact. Sayings like "You're a game-changer" or "You've left a lasting legacy" should be reserved for moments of truly extraordinary value or transformation.

While the chart offers a helpful structure, it's only a starting point. Adjust the language to fit your style and make it authentic to you. The goal is to have meaningful and impactful words ready so that when you see excellence, you can deliver praise that inspires motivation and confidence in others. Recognition, when intentional and authentic, builds trust, engagement, and momentum. It's one of the simplest yet most effective ways to bring out the best in your team. Don't underestimate the power of words—they can make all the difference.

Recognition Best Practice – Be Creative

One of my favorite lessons in creative recognition came from an executive who truly understood the power of personal touches. It was Christmastime, and instead of sending the usual cards or bonuses, he did something extraordinary. Knowing how much family meant to his team, he sent cards directly to their kids. Each card included $100 and a handwritten note saying, "Thank you for allowing your mom/dad to travel for their job. I know it's hard when they're away from home." Rather than simply rewarding his team, he made the gesture deeply personal, showing a level of thoughtfulness that resonated far beyond the money.

Another example came from a coachee of mine. One day, he overheard a superintendent on his construction site mention that he'd accidentally left his nine-iron on the green over the weekend. Instead of a standard thank-you bonus, my coachee went a step further. Knowing the superintendent was an avid golfer, he purchased a replacement nine-iron. When he presented it as a token of appreciation for the superintendent's recent late nights and hard work, the recipient was nearly in tears. The gesture wasn't just about the golf club—it showed that my coachee listened, cared, and understood him on a personal level.

The Power of Personal Touch

These stories illustrate a simple truth: recognition doesn't have to be grandiose—it just needs to be personal. A thoughtful gesture can have a lasting impact, no matter how small. Consider writing a heartfelt note, giving tickets to an event they'd love, or even posting a meaningful shoutout on LinkedIn. It's not the size of the gesture but the care behind it that makes it memorable.

Servant Leaders know that creative recognition goes beyond motivation; it builds loyalty and strengthens relationships. When people feel seen and valued in meaningful ways, their connection to the team and organization grows exponentially.

Serving the Need for Recognition

Recognition is often the lowest-hanging fruit of Servant Leadership. It doesn't require extraordinary effort—just paying attention to the good around you and acting on it. Use the right language, personalize your approach, and deliver recognition in a way that resonates with the individual. Done well, recognition serves as "free motivation," sustaining your team's energy and commitment.

Make a habit of passing credit along to your team for every success. Build trust and credibility through consistent positive reinforcement so that when it's time for constructive feedback, it's more likely to be received openly. Recognition is a simple but powerful tool—don't overlook its potential. Commit to helping others feel appreciated, and watch the difference it makes in your team's engagement and performance.

Self-Assess

How consistent are you at "looking for the good" on your team?

1-----------2------------3------------4------------5------------6------------7

I focus mostly on the problems and challenges	I consistently notice things going right and recognize it

How do you react when someone praises you and your team?

1-----------2------------3------------4------------5------------6------------7

I thank them for appreciating my talents	I immediately share credit and highlight key contributors' efforts

How well do you maintain a 3/1 feedback ratio?

1-----------2------------3------------4------------5------------6------------7

I tend to give very little positive but lots of constructive feedback	I give lots of positive feedback so my constructive feedback is better received

How articulate is your praise, gratitude, and appreciation?

1-----------2------------3------------4------------5------------6------------7

I struggle to find the right words or use the same language repeatedly	I have a deep vocabulary that appropriately validates effort

Scoring:

24-28 = Congrats! You are likely skillful at recognizing your people and sustaining high levels of motivation

13-23 = Your team likely feels their efforts are sometimes noticed, yet there is room to improve your recognition skills

4-12 = Recognition may be an underserved need on your team

Reflect

How do you like to receive recognition? To what extent might your preferences influence how you recognize others?

Who on your team is due for recognition right now? How can you creatively show your appreciation?

What's the most difficult part of recognizing others as a leader?

a. Noticing good work and not dismissing it as routine
b. Finding the time to offer recognition
c. Striking the right balance to avoid over- or underdoing it
d. Finding the right words to say or write

How can you be more consistent with offering recognition?

Recap

- Recognition is a leadership responsibility, not a nice-to-have. It fuels performance, trust, and engagement.
- Recognition is often overlooked due to flawed mindsets like "they're just doing their job" or "too much praise loses impact."
- Servant Leaders "look for the good" daily—acknowledging both big wins and small contributions that support team culture.
- The Golden Rule of Recognition: always pass credit to those who earned it—promptly and publicly when appropriate.
- Use the 3-to-1 feedback ratio (positive to constructive) to build trust and increase receptivity to improvement conversations.
- Language matters—elevate praise to match the level of contribution, from everyday gratitude to legacy-level appreciation.
- Customize recognition—some want public acknowledgment, others prefer private.
- Get creative and personal with how you recognize others; thoughtful, unexpected gestures leave lasting impressions.

SERVING THE TEAM

"When you're surrounded by people who share a passionate commitment around a common purpose, anything is possible."

— Howard Schultz

11

THE NEED FOR DIRECTION

"Whoa...Did you see that? Did that really just happen?" I cried out to my fellow Army Officers as the first images of an airplane smashing into the World Trade Center flashed across CNN on our office television. The room was abuzz. We all responded similarly to what we were witnessing: a combination of amazement, disbelief, and immature exuberance. But when the second aircraft struck the South Tower, everything changed. Our shock turned to realization: life as we knew it would never be the same.

"Gentlemen, get a hold of yourselves! Don't you realize our nation is under attack? This is an act of war—start preparing yourself now!" Lieutenant Colonel Michael Spencer's commanding voice cut through the chaos, refocusing the room. His words provided the immediate direction we needed. But questions lingered: Prepare to fight who? Where? When? And how will we win?

Over the following months, some answers would emerge—though they often led to more questions. While Special Operations Forces began operations in Afghanistan, I transferred to 1-1 CAV, a Divisional Armored Cavalry Squadron stationed near Frankfurt, Germany. It was a dream assignment. I'd be taking command of an elite unit with a historical lineage dating back to 1833. Since the early 1950s, 1-1 CAV's mission had remained largely unchanged: protect U.S. interests in Europe. For decades, this meant training to stop the Soviet forces from invading Germany during a hypothetical WWIII—a focus that suddenly felt antiquated in the wake of 9/11.

Rapid Adaptation

Within weeks of my arrival, the political climate shifted dramatically. Attention turned from Afghanistan to Iraq, with a growing focus on weapons of mass destruction. Soon, it became clear that a more conventional war was imminent. Armor and infantry units would be critical to defeating the world's third-largest army. Given Germany's proximity to Iraq, our division was likely to be among the first deployed. The countdown began.

Our squadron faced an overwhelming transformation. The green camouflage of our vehicles and uniforms—a perfect metaphor for our outdated Cold War-era preparation—needed to be replaced with desert-ready tan. But the challenge ran much deeper than a change of paint. We were about to lead soldiers into urban combat against an unconventional enemy in one of the Middle East's densest population centers. It was the polar opposite of the open European countryside engagements we had trained for. We needed to unlearn outdated tactics, rapidly master new skills, and prepare our soldiers for a different kind of combat. The stakes were enormous. Failing to adapt fast enough meant soldiers might not make it home.

The next sixty days became a blur of intense preparation as Staff Officers sprang into action to support Troop Commanders. The S-2 (Intelligence Officer) established a SCIF (secret compartmentalized information facility) to assess the terrain and track enemy movements via satellite imagery. Our S-4 (Logistics Officer) issued new uniforms, procured needed war supplies, repainted our vehicles, and coordinated railhead operations to load our equipment on the ships. The S-1 (Personnel Officer) ensured critical administration, such as wills, next of kin, and flight manifests, was taken care of. The S-3 (Operations Officer) and Squadron Executive Officer would plan and execute short-notice weapons qualification events. The Squadron and Deputy Commander would be involved in ceaseless Divisional and Brigade level deployment and war planning meetings.

Embracing New Roles

I served as an Assistant Operations Officer at the time, working alongside an outstanding team of fellow Captains. Thanks to previous experience, I was asked to lead an unusual effort. As a young lieutenant in Texas, my Commander had previously served in a Ranger Battalion. For him to move from an elite light infantry unit to a heavy armor unit was unheard of. Yet, it proved fortuitous as he cross-trained me well in advanced infantry skills. Thus, I became the de facto "expert" on urban infantry operations, tasked with training Tankers and Scouts in skills like reflexive firing, clearing a room, establishing checkpoints, and even non-lethal crowd control procedures.

Despite the gravity of our mission, this was one of the best periods of my career. We had a blast! Whereas peacetime training took months of planning, coordination, and approvals, we were given resources almost immediately and free rein to make things happen. We qualified weapon systems on previously inaccessible German ranges, trained for day and night operations in mock cities, and even learned basic Arabic for engaging local populations.

Perhaps the most formidable challenge wasn't mastering the infantry skills but shifting a lifetime of tanker mentality. Tankers—accustomed to staying in their vehicles—were notorious for the mantra "death before dismount." Convincing them to embrace dismounted operations wasn't easy, but professionalism prevailed. When we deployed to Kuwait, we had transformed into a unit that could rival any mechanized infantry force.

VUCA = Volatility, Uncertainty, Complexity, Ambiguity

This story illustrates the essence of VUCA—Volatility, Uncertainty, Complexity, and Ambiguity. For years, our unit had trained for conventional, predictable threats in Europe. Suddenly, the 9/11 attacks thrust us into an entirely new reality. We found ourselves in the urban environment of Baghdad, Iraq, fighting against an asymmetrical and erratic enemy.

During this tumultuous period, the U.S. Military first coined the term VUCA to better describe the new, unpredictable, fast-changing environment it was facing. The concept has since spread to corporate boardrooms as businesses grapple with their own forms of disruption.

> **"As we know, there are known knowns; there are things we know we know. We also know there are known unknowns; that is to say we know there are some things we do not know. But there are also unknown unknowns—the ones we don't know we don't know."**
>
> - *U.S. Secretary of Defense Donald Rumsfeld (2002)*

Let's unpack VUCA-what it means and how it shows up today.

Volatility refers to unexpected challenges of unknown duration. Yet, it's not necessarily hard to understand. Knowledge about the challenge is available. Example: Gas prices spike due to the war in Ukraine and a Russian oil boycott. We don't know how long the war and increased pricing will last, but we understand what led to the tension and how boycotts impact gas pricing.

Uncertainty - Despite a lack of information, basic cause and effect are known. Change is possible...but not a given. Example: Apple launches its newest iPhone with never before seen technology, muddying the future market share potential of rival competitors. Samsung knows Apple's new technology is going to steal market share but doesn't know how long it will be before it can launch a similarly competitive product.

Complexity - Situations with many connected parts and variables. Prediction is possible, yet the pure volume or nature of it can be overwhelming. Example: Southwest Airlines opens flights to Brazil, now requiring them to deal with different regulatory laws, tariffs, and cultural values. This is a solvable challenge, but it will require various expertise and time due to its complexity.

Ambiguity - Causal relationships are unclear, and no precedent exists. You face "unknown unknowns." Example: A new super virus could emerge and impact the world even more than COVID-19 did. This dilemma has no solution yet, as we don't know anything about the virus or how it emerges.

Adapted from Bennett, N., & Lamoine, G. J. (2014). What vuca really means for you. *Harvard Business Review*, (January-February).

As you read this, you've likely drawn parallels to how VUCA affects your own industry. The truth is that VUCA is here to stay—and its pace is accelerating. That's why providing direction has become an essential leadership skill. Leaders must learn to "VUCA Proof©" themselves and their organizations to meet the critical needs of their teams.

To support leaders, I developed my VUCA Proof© model below.

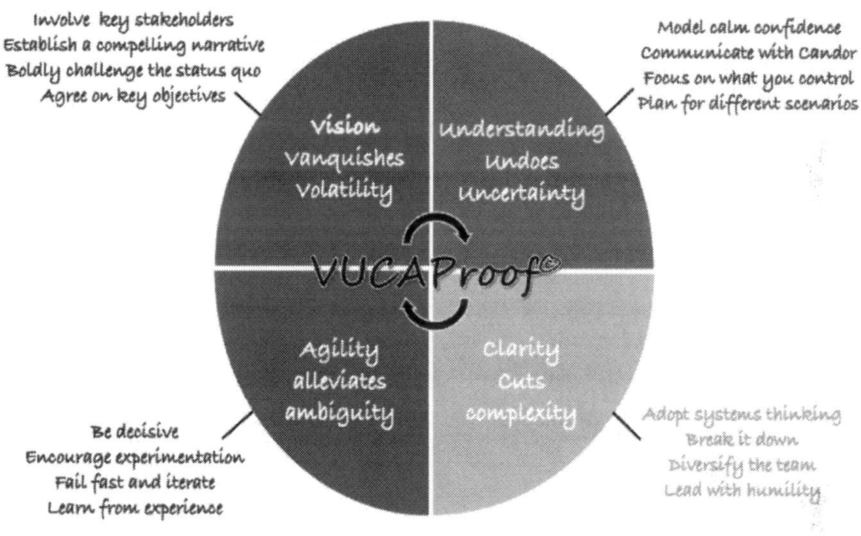

Vision Vanquishes Volatility

During my deployment to Iraq, our unit successfully reinvented itself during an exceptionally volatile time. How did we manage this? The short answer is that failure was not an option, but the reality is more nuanced. Our success hinged on a shared vision and total alignment in executing our plan. Thankfully, we had exceptional senior leadership who understood how to provide clear direction in uncertain times. They saw where we needed to go, defined success, and challenged us to figure out how to achieve it. Everyone knew their role, believed in the mission, and understood why change was essential. While we may have been maneuvering upstream, we overcame the current by everyone rowing hard in the same direction.

Casting a vision is one of a leader's most significant responsibilities. When leaders articulate a clear vision, goals, and expectations, they create alignment and inspire collective action. Contrast this with a directionless team, where dysfunction quickly emerges—anxiety, confusion, and indecision take hold, distractions multiply, conflict arises, and morale plummets. Without vision and direction, chaos thrives, especially in volatile environments. Servant Leaders understand this and ensure their teams have the clarity and purpose needed to act decisively.

Crafting a Compelling Vision

The concept of vision might seem daunting—like leaders must be soothsayers who can gaze into the future. The good news is that crafting a vision shouldn't be a solo endeavor. A best practice is to involve the team in co-creating the vision. Help them to identify the potential challenges ahead, then ask what adaptations are needed to be successful. At its core, vision is a call for adaptation. Leaders must establish a compelling narrative about why the status quo is unacceptable and why change is necessary. An excellent vision inspires the team to envision a better future and aligns their actions toward achieving it.

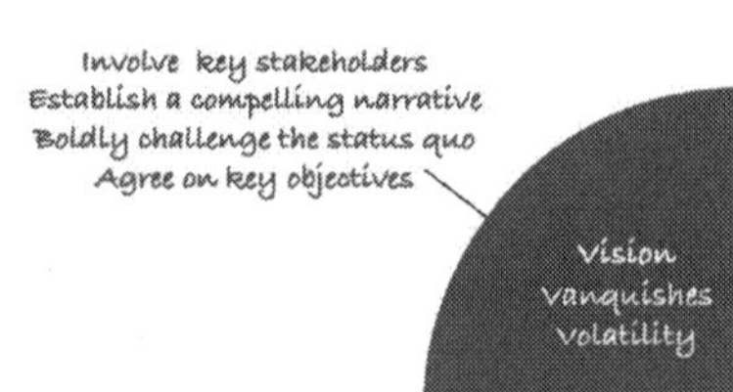

To co-create a powerful vision with your team, ask them:

- What impact do we want to make as a team, both internally and externally?
- What would that look like if we were wildly successful three years from now?
- What challenges could get in our way of being successful?
- What changes are necessary to adapt to the demands of these challenges?
- What unique strengths do we bring as a team that can drive the organization forward?
- What bold but achievable goals should we aim for in the next 12-24 months?
- What would make this vision personally meaningful and motivating for each of us?

Encourage bold thinking while pragmatically addressing concerns. Integrating team input fosters ownership and ensures buy-in when the vision is finalized.

Communicating the Vision

When casting your vision to your broader team and stakeholders, remember that good leaders give directions, and great leaders give direction. Direction is the destination, while directions are the path to get there. Paint a vivid picture of the outcome—help your team see and feel what success looks like. Describe what they will notice and the emotions they will experience once the vision becomes a reality. A good vision is concise, memorable, and emotionally resonant. If your team can't easily recall the vision's essence, it's unlikely to inspire action.

When presenting your vision, the goal is to secure buy-in and alignment. By involving your team in the process, you've already laid the groundwork for acceptance. Still, encourage feedback and debate to address any lingering doubts. It's better to resolve resistance upfront than face passive disengagement later. For leaders of leaders, establish a consistent communication plan to ensure your vision cascades effectively through the organization. Your team can weather even the most volatile challenges with everyone aligned and moving together.

Understanding Undoes Uncertainty

Once the vision is clear, the hard work of execution begins. While you may have a broad plan established, no plan is perfect because the future is full of uncertainties. Uncertainty breeds anxiety, and an anxious team becomes slow and ineffective. Servant Leaders recognize the need to settle this unease by fostering understanding and providing reassurance.

Modeling Calm Confidence

Servant Leaders act as emotional anchors by modeling the energy that's missing in their teams. If the team feels uneasy, the leader must exude steadiness. If nervousness arises, the leader projects poise. This can be challenging, especially when the leader shares those feelings.

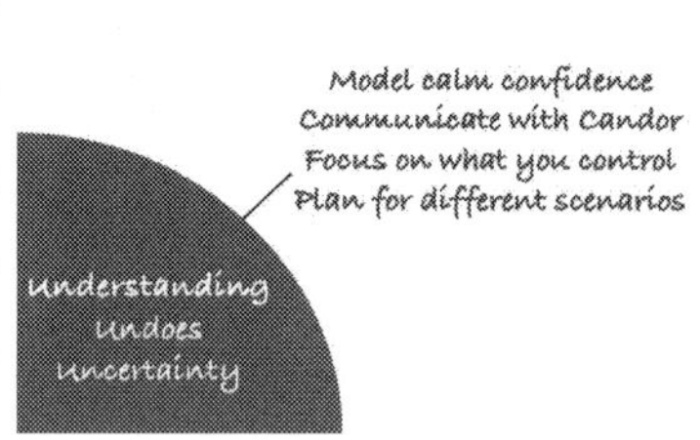

After all, leaders are humans and aren't immune to feeling anxious, too. If you find yourself in this situation, remind yourself, *"If not you, then who?"* Someone needs to demonstrate to the team how to respond collectively. Know that a leader's energy is contagious. Show any uneasiness about future uncertainty, and that energy will cascade throughout your team. Instead, deliberately model calm confidence, and you'll inspire your team to adopt a similar composure.

Speak with Candor and Focus on Controllables

In uncertain times, communicating with candor and focusing on what you can control is critical. I once coached a leader managing a development team at an AI startup. During our engagement, his company unexpectedly laid off some employees, which created a tumultuous working environment. Suddenly, all my coachee's priority tasks seemed moot as his team wondered if they would be next to get the axe. The anxiety was crippling and threatened his team's productivity, so we devised a plan.

On our coaching calls, I encouraged him to listen deeply to his team's concerns and help his people feel heard. Validating their emotions was an important first step in returning the team to productivity. We then focused on communicating with more candor. He worked to collect as much factual information as possible from executive-level leadership and then transparently shared what he could. Knowing the hard truth is always better than having a team fill voids of information with their own assumptions. His actions help dispel rumors and reduce anxiety.

Finally, I assisted him in refocusing his team on what they could control. No one could control how future layoffs might impact the team. However, they could work to influence those decisions by working hard and performing at a high level. The message to his team was clear: "We may not know what's next, but let's make ourselves indispensable by delivering exceptional results." In a time of great uncertainty, my coachee served his team by providing critical direction. This approach rallied the team, transforming fear into focus and preserving their jobs.

Planning for Uncertainty

Contingency planning is one of the most powerful ways to mitigate uncertainty. In the Army, every plan we made included contingencies. We constantly asked:

- What's the most likely scenario?
- What's the worst-case scenario?
- What's Plan B if the worst-case scenario happens?
- What's Plan C if an unforeseen scenario emerges?

By defining these options ahead of time, we ensured that when circumstances changed—as they inevitably did—we could adapt quickly and decisively. Business leaders can apply this same approach by "wargaming" potential outcomes and building decision trees. For example:

- If our new product launch doesn't generate $150K in revenue within the first month, we'll shift our ad strategy and lower the price by 10%.
- If Project A is three days behind schedule, we'll work overtime for a week to catch up. If we're still behind after a week, we'll reallocate two team members from Project B to support it.

This level of preparation has multiple benefits. It instills confidence, reduces anxiety, and ensures your team is equipped to handle unexpected challenges. Additionally, it enhances operational efficiency—when decision points are clearly defined and criteria for action are established, teams operate with greater autonomy, processes become standardized, and outcomes become more predictable.

The best leaders don't just react to change—they anticipate it. And when the unexpected happens, a well-prepared team won't hesitate. They'll already know what to do.

Clarity Cuts Complexity

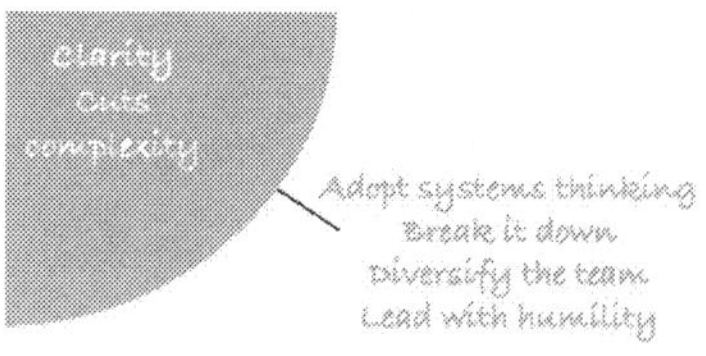

If you were born before 1990, you probably remember a simpler time—before smartphones, social media, artificial intelligence, or even the internet. While these technologies undoubtedly improved our lives in many ways, they also made life significantly more complex. For those born after 1990, this complexity is all they've ever known. By the time they entered the workforce, technology was already fully integrated into daily life, making complexity the new normal. In today's fast-paced world, this presents a challenge for leaders tasked with providing direction amidst overwhelming distractions and information overload. What teams need now is clarity—a leader who can step back, see the bigger picture, and refocus their energy on what truly matters.

Adopting a Systems Thinking Mindset

The first step to cutting through complexity is adopting a systems thinking mindset. "Systems thinking is a way of making sense of the complexity of the world by looking at it in terms of wholes and relationships rather than by splitting it down into its parts."[20] This approach is crucial in environments where everything is interconnected and interdependent.

In my coaching work, I often hear executives express a desire to "think more strategically." What they're really seeking is the ability to analyze situations, understand relationships, anticipate outcomes, and develop coherent strategies—all of which require systems thinking. While junior and mid-level leaders are adept at solving discrete problems, senior leaders must be able to see how different elements interact within a larger system. But how can leaders develop this ability? Here are three tangible ways for leaders to practice systems thinking.

1. **Map Out Cause-and-Effect Relationships** – Use mind maps to visualize how different factors influence each other in your organization.
   Example: If employee burnout rises, map contributing factors (e.g., workload,

poor delegation, unclear priorities) and see where interventions can break negative cycles.

2. **Encourage Cross-Functional Collaboration** - Break down silos by fostering open dialogue between different departments or teams.
   Example: Have engineering, sales, and customer success teams meet regularly to discuss interdependencies and share perspectives on how one group's work affects the others.
3. **Use Data to Identify Patterns Over Time** - Instead of reacting to individual problems, track trends and systemic patterns using dashboards or historical data.
   Example: If customer churn is increasing, look beyond isolated complaints—analyze long-term satisfaction scores, service response times, and product adoption rates.

Breaking Problems into Manageable Parts

Another powerful strategy for navigating complexity is "chunking," or breaking down large problems into smaller, more manageable parts. When a team feels overwhelmed and stuck, a Servant Leader steps in to simplify the challenge. By dividing the problem into smaller subproblems, you help your team focus on immediate priorities. This approach builds momentum through small wins, reigniting energy and optimism for tackling the bigger issue.

Effective chunking starts with identifying the root problem. In complex environments, teams often misdiagnose the issue, wasting time and resources on the wrong solutions. A simple but effective tool for problem diagnosis is the *Five Whys*. Start by asking, "Why did this happen?" Continue asking "why" to each subsequent answer until you uncover the root cause. You typically gain improved clarity by the time you've asked your fifth "why," but more complex problems may require you to keep going. For example:

1. **Why did we lose this client?**
   They were unhappy with service delays.

2. **Why were there service delays?**
   We're understaffed for their account.
3. **Why are we understaffed?**
   Open positions haven't been filled.
4. **Why haven't they been filled?**
   Our hiring process is too slow.
5. **Why is the hiring process slow?**
   We lack dedicated recruiting resources.

This exercise reveals that our real problem isn't lost revenue due to service delays; it's a hiring bottleneck. As a leader, you might prioritize fixing the recruitment process instead of improving service to achieve the best return on effort.

Embracing Diverse Perspectives

Complexity demands diversity in team composition. It's well-documented that diverse teams consistently outperform homogenous ones. A 2023 McKinsey report found that companies in the top quartile for ethnic diversity are 39% more likely to outperform those in the bottom quartile.[21] Why? Because diverse teams bring varied perspectives, reducing blind spots and increasing innovation.

Homogenous teams are more prone to groupthink, where everyone agrees too quickly, often leading to flawed decisions. In contrast, diverse teams challenge assumptions and generate a broader range of ideas, which is invaluable when addressing complex problems. As a leader, prioritize hiring and fostering diversity, and not just demographic diversity (age, gender, ethnicity, etc.). Hire also for diverse backgrounds, skillsets, personalities, and educational experiences. Emphasizing diversity isn't just good ethics; it's smart strategy. Adding new perspectives, talents, and ways of thinking will help generate potential solutions that were previously imperceptible.

Modeling Humility and Curiosity

Finally, Servant Leaders tackle complexity by modeling humility and curiosity. No matter how experienced or knowledgeable a leader is, a single person cannot solve complex problems. Instead of trying to provide answers, a humble leader asks insightful questions that encourage group learning.

Facilitating meaningful dialogue among team members helps uncover insights that no individual could reach alone. However, this requires a balance of influence and openness. In meetings, it's common to see individuals jockeying to prove they're the "smartest person in the room." Talented people like to share their experience and expertise, but this can be unproductive when solving complex problems. As the leader, you must set the tone by demonstrating humility, fostering curiosity, and encouraging collaboration. When you model this behavior, your team will follow suit, and solutions will emerge from collective intelligence rather than individual ego.

Agility Alleviates Ambiguity

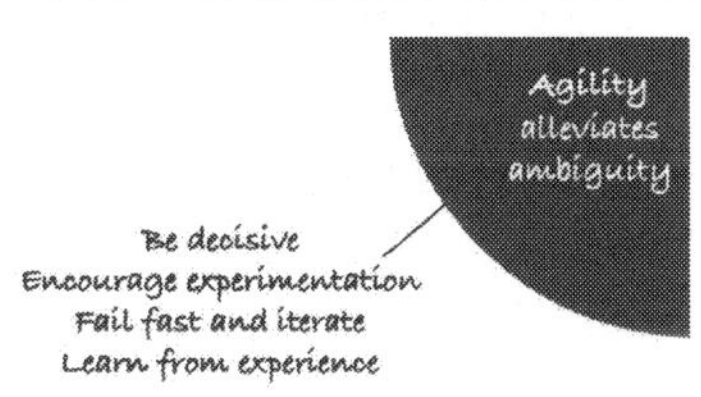

The final element of VUCA—ambiguity—is arguably the most challenging of all. Leaders can't prepare for "unknown unknowns," and there's often no precedent to guide decision-making once these unknowns materialize. Unlike volatility, uncertainty, or complexity, which allow some level of proactive management, ambiguity keeps leaders on their heels and in reactive mode. However, while leaders can't avoid being reactive, they can prepare for *how* they'll react. Operating in ambiguity requires leaders to assess situations as best they can, accept risks, experiment, learn quickly, and adjust. Collectively, these skills form agility—the ability to adapt and respond swiftly to changing environments.

To illustrate how agility alleviates ambiguity, I'll share a short story from my time serving in Iraq.

Baghdad, Iraq – August 2003

It was a scorching summer day as a small team of soldiers prepared to leave Camp Slayer, our base of operations and a former Saddam Hussein palace repurposed as Squadron Headquarters. The mission was simple: a routine resupply run. The S-4 team needed additional personnel for security, and as a staff officer who spent most of my time in planning cells, I jumped at the chance to "get outside the wire." My team of eager Non-Commissioned Officers (NCOs) and enlisted soldiers felt the same. We volunteered enthusiastically, unaware of what lay ahead.

Dressed in heavy body armor, Kevlar helmets, and tactical vests loaded with ammunition, we sweated under the weight of our gear. As we lined up our convoy to exit the base, the gate guard stopped us. "Sir, before you go, I need to brief you on this," he said, handing me a printed slide. The image showed what looked like an artillery shell buried in the ground with wires protruding. "This is their new weapon of choice. Watch out for this!" he warned.

It was our first introduction to an IED (Improvised Explosive Device), a term now synonymous with modern warfare. Back then, it was a relatively unknown threat, and that one slide was the extent of our training.

As we swiftly darted down the highway towards the heart of the city, the oppressively hot air felt like someone holding a hair dryer directly in your face. We reached the Baghdad marketplace without incident, settling into the familiar rhythm of bartering with merchants. This was a different time in Iraq—one where we could walk the streets relatively freely, stopping for a falafel and tea. With supplies loaded, we began our journey back to base.

Then, it happened.

A deafening explosion rocked the convoy, jolting me forward in my seat. My mind flashed to the IED briefing we'd received, and a sinking realization set in. Grabbing the radio, I called for a status check. Fortunately, everyone in our convoy was unharmed. But as we surveyed the scene, we spotted a U.S. vehicle burning on the opposite side of the road. Another convoy had been hit.

The question wasn't if we should help—it was how. None of us were trained in responding to an IED attack, but we'd heard secondary bombs were often planted to target rescuers. As the ranking officer, I had to provide some direction quickly.

After consulting with my NCOs, we decided to dismount and cross the road to assist. By the time we reached the scene, other soldiers had already pulled the injured crew from the burning vehicle and were administering first aid. But trouble was brewing—a crowd of curious locals began gathering. Soon, about 50 people were within 10 meters of us, and it was impossible to know if they were innocent onlookers or potential threats. We needed to take control of the situation.

I ordered our team to establish a perimeter, but the language barrier and heightened emotions made crowd control challenging. Tensions flared. Soldiers grew visibly agitated, some raising their weapons in fear and frustration. The situation teetered on the edge of chaos.

Then, I noticed our vulnerability: a nearby highway overpass. If enemy combatants were among the crowd, the overpass would give them a clear vantage point and open fields of fire onto all of us. I quickly redirected some soldiers to secure it, creating near-side and far-side security. This elevated position allowed us to monitor the scene more effectively and eased some of the tension.

With the immediate danger mitigated, I shifted focus to calming our team and defusing hostilities with the crowd. Walking the perimeter, I checked in with each soldier, offering reassurance and steadying their nerves. Thankfully, our collective professionalism prevailed, and within 20 minutes, reinforcements arrived to evacuate the wounded. We collapsed our perimeter and returned to base without further incident.

The Power of Agility

How was our team able to handle such an ambiguous and high-stakes situation? We barely knew what an I.E.D. was, much less how to react to one. It was our agility—our capacity to adapt, decide, and act in the face of the unknown—that made the difference.

Agility begins with decisiveness. Ambiguity often leads to "analysis paralysis," where fear of making the wrong decision results in no decision at all. Leaders must overcome this tendency by embracing purposeful action over perfection. To help identify barriers to decisiveness, I've outlined four common "**Desires That Degrade Decisiveness**":

1. **The Desire to Be Perfect** – Poor decision-making can make us feel

incompetent and inadequate, negatively impacting our ego and self-esteem. This can be a strong motivator to avoid making decisions until we are certain we're correct. Yet, mistakes in life are unavoidable. Decisive leaders accept vulnerability and prioritize progress over ego protection.

2. **The Desire to Please Everyone** – Leaders make decisions that impact others, so they often want consensus to achieve maximum buy-in. Decisive leaders know consensus is ideal but rarely achievable. They balance listening to input with making tough calls, even if it means disappointing some.
3. **The Desire for More Data** – In a world where leaders can access instant and unlimited data, many still complain, "I don't have enough information to make a decision yet." Then, they compile more data and do more analysis. Decision-making can be difficult, and having our options open feels good. Yet, delaying decisions just delays outcomes and learning. Decisive leaders recognize when they have enough data to act and prioritize learning through action.
4. **The Desire to Avoid Consequences** – Big decisions carry risks with potential consequences. Perhaps jobs are on the line, or significant financial risks are at stake. The pressure can cause leaders to delay decision-making. Courageous leaders weigh options, mitigate risks, and move forward decisively when others are unwilling to step up to the challenge.

My I.E.D. story is a good illustration of how agile leaders treat decisions as experiments. Every choice provided valuable feedback—either confirming a hypothesis or revealing areas for adjustment. For example, my decision to form our perimeter without securing the overpass was a poor one. But it was still a better decision than doing nothing—sitting in our vehicles and failing to secure the incident at all. By experimenting, failing fast, and iterating, we accelerated our path to success. When leaders reframe failures as learning opportunities, they free themselves and their teams from the fear of making mistakes. This shift in mindset fosters decisiveness and agility as the norm.

Serving the Need for Direction

Providing direction in today's VUCA world is no small feat. Leaders must equip themselves with tools to navigate volatility, uncertainty, complexity, and ambiguity. By casting a vision that withstands volatility, fostering understanding to calm uncertainty, creating clarity to simplify complexity, and embracing agility to manage ambiguity, Servant Leaders prepare their teams to meet the challenges of a rapidly evolving world.

Self-Assess

How skilled are you at casting a vision that provides direction?

1-----------2-----------3-----------4-----------5-----------6-----------7

It's not something I have much experience with — I involve the team and create urgency for bold changes

How well do you and your team handle future uncertainty?

1-----------2-----------3-----------4-----------5-----------6-----------7

Uncertainty rattles us, and we tend to be reactive — We are poised in uncertain times and plan contingencies

How skilled are you at providing clarity in complex situations?

1-----------2-----------3-----------4-----------5-----------6-----------7

I can get overwhelmed and miss important connections — I'm a systems thinker who models curiosity and humility

How well does your team operate in ambiguous situations?

1-----------2-----------3-----------4-----------5-----------6-----------7

We suffer from paralysis analysis and failure to act — We act decisively, experiment with options, fail fast, and learn

Scoring:

24-28 = Congrats! You are one of the few leaders who can provide sufficient direction to their teams when operating in a VUCA world

13-23 = Your team likely has enough direction to thrive in some but not all situations

4-12 = Direction may be an underserved need on your team; check to see where you can enhance vision, understanding, clarity, or agility

Reflect

Think about the last time your team faced significant volatility, uncertainty, complexity, or ambiguity. How did you react? What would you do differently today if you faced the same situation?

Which of the "Desires that Degrade Decisiveness" show up the most for you when making tough decisions?

a. The Desire to Be Perfect
b. The Desire to Please Everyone
c. The Desire for More Data
d. The Desire to Avoid Consequences

Recap

- VUCA—Volatility, Uncertainty, Complexity, Ambiguity—is increasing exponentially. Leaders must "VUCA Proof©" themselves and their teams.
- Vision Vanquishes Volatility
  - A compelling vision aligns teams and drives action during chaos
  - Co-create vision with your team to foster ownership and buy-in
  - Great leaders give direction, not directions
- Understanding Undoes Uncertainty
  - Leaders calm anxious teams by modeling calm confidence
  - Speak with candor, validate concerns, and focus on controllables
  - Use contingency planning to reduce decision fatigue
- Clarity Cuts Complexity
  - Use systems thinking and break big problems into manageable parts
  - Embrace team diversity to avoid blind spots and innovate
  - Model humility by asking questions instead of having all the answers
- Agility Alleviates Ambiguity
  - Leaders adapt, learn, and respond swiftly to the unknown
  - Be decisive and act—decisions are experiments, not final answers
  - Let go of perfection, people-pleasing, over-analysis, and fear of consequences to foster agility

12

THE NEED FOR PROTECTION

Some deerskin wrapped around your feet shields you from the sharp rocks as you walk a familiar trail. Layers of fur offer some protection against the elements, but as night falls, the dropping temperature makes you long for the warmth of a fire. Soon, you hear your clan in the distance, and the smell of smoke reaches you through the cool night air. You're almost home. A wave of relief washes over you because being with the clan means safety from predators. You begin to unwind as you take refuge in the damp cave, warmed by the fire's light. After sharing a meal with your family, your eyes grow heavy, and you drift off to sleep.

Suddenly, a commotion jolts you awake! Disoriented, you struggle to understand what's happening. The lookout is sounding the alarm—danger is near. It's a bear, massive and hungry, rearing up on its hind legs and growling. Fear grips you. Instinctively, you turn to the clan's leader. So does everyone else. The leader, experienced and decisive, immediately grabs his spear and rallies the group. Together, they fend off the bear with torches and rocks until it retreats into the darkness. The leader's quick actions reinforce his status, and the clan withdraws safely back into the cave.

Protection Then and Now

This scene could have played out 100,000 years ago in an early hunter-gatherer society. Back then, the need for protection was primal. Leaders earned trust by keeping the group safe through personal strength, organizational skills, or the ability to build coalitions. The social contract was simple: the leader enjoyed perks like access to food and mates as long as they fulfilled their role. Failure to keep the group safe meant losing status—and being replaced.

Fast forward to today, and while we no longer face wild bears in the night, our primal need for protection remains. The threats have changed, but our stress responses haven't. Today's "bear" might be an angry Vice President demanding answers about missed performance metrics. If the blame falls on you, it could mean missed promotions—or worse, losing your job. And with bills piling up, the threat feels as real as any predator.

In these moments, we still instinctively look to our leaders for protection. The stakes may have shifted, but the expectation hasn't. So, how does a modern leader provide protection in today's workplace?

Protecting Focus

Every organization striving for big goals will encounter obstacles. Limited resources, poor communication, and internal resistance to change are common challenges, but distraction is the biggest threat to progress today. Leaders in my coaching practice frequently tell me how hard it is to keep their teams focused. In today's workplaces, people are often stretched thin, firefighting constant "emergencies" and struggling under dotted-line reporting structures and cross-functional matrices.

This frantic environment leads to burnout. When everything is treated as urgent, priorities blur, and meaningful progress stalls. Servant Leaders recognize this chaos and step in to protect their teams from distractions. For example, if a dotted-line manager tries to reprioritize one of their team members' efforts, a Servant Leader will advocate to keep their priorities intact. If upper leadership sends an "urgent" request for a detailed presentation, Servant Leaders don't drop everything and start building slides full of data. They evaluate whether the request warrants interruption and pushback if necessary.

The Army has a saying: "No combat-ready unit ever passed inspection." It's a reminder to focus on what truly matters instead of getting bogged down in tasks that don't align with your ultimate objectives. Servant Leaders apply this principle in the workplace, prioritizing their team's highest-value work and shielding them from unnecessary interruptions.

Communicating Trade-offs

Protecting your team doesn't mean saying "no" to every request—it's about communicating trade-offs. For example, if your manager asks your team to take on a new task, you might respond, "We can do that, but it will delay our current deliverables by a week. Are you okay with that trade-off?" This approach forces others to weigh the cost of their requests and often leads to more thoughtful decisions. When everything is a priority, then nothing is a priority. Servant Leaders protect the team by challenging knee-jerk reactions, holding their ground, and maintaining focus.

The Art of Prioritization

Protecting focus starts with knowing what to protect. Without clear priorities, leaders risk getting pulled into a short-term mindset where the loudest or most recent demand becomes the "priority." Servant Leaders use tools like the *Eisenhower Matrix* to distinguish between urgent and important tasks versus those that can be scheduled, delegated, or eliminated.

Dwight Eisenhower lived one of the most productive lives in history. He was a two-term President of the United States who was responsible for the Interstate Highway System. He was a five-star General in the U.S. Army responsible for Allied Forces in Europe during World War II. He also "served as President of Columbia University, became the first Supreme Commander of NATO, and somehow found time to pursue hobbies like golfing and oil painting."[22] He attributed his productivity to his strategy for deciding how to organize tasks best. His approach has been studied and validated for generations now, and while the *Eisenhower Matrix* was initially intended to help with personal productivity, I've reformatted it to support team prioritization.

The Eisenhower Matrix for Team Productivity

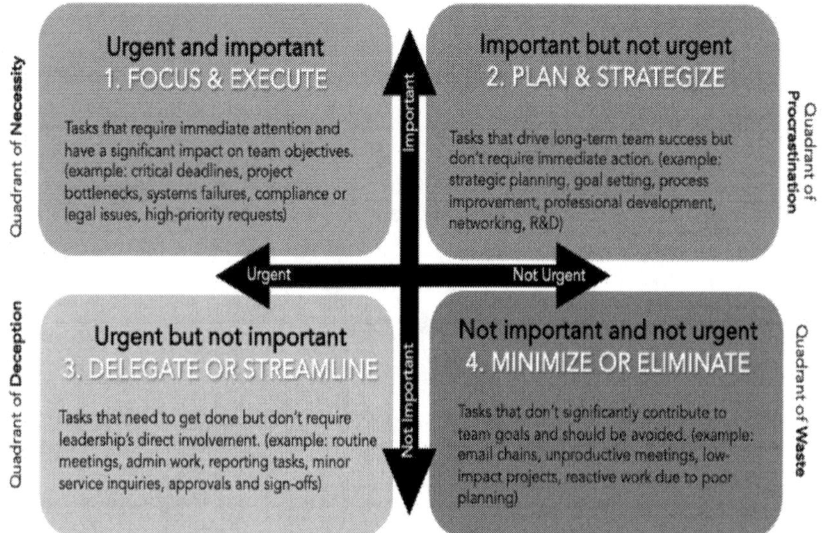

To implement the *Eisenhower Matrix*, meet with your team once a week and evaluate which quadrant collective tasks belong.

Quadrant 1 (Top Left): **Urgent & Important**

FOCUS & EXECUTE

Tasks that require immediate attention and have a significant impact on team objectives.

- Critical client deadlines
- Major project bottlenecks that need resolution
- Urgent system failures or outages
- Compliance or legal issues that must be addressed
- High-priority stakeholder requests with tight deadlines

Quadrant 2 (Top Right): **Important but Not Urgent**

PLAN & STRATEGIZE

Tasks that drive long-term team success but don't require immediate action.

- Strategic planning and goal-setting
- Process improvement initiatives
- Leadership development and team training
- Innovation projects and R&D efforts
- Building cross-functional relationships

Quadrant 3 (Bottom Left): **Urgent but Not Important DELEGATE OR STREAMLINE**

Tasks that need to get done but don't require leadership's direct involvement.

- Status update meetings and routine check-ins
- Low-priority administrative work
- Repetitive reporting tasks that can be automated
- Minor customer service inquiries
- Internal approvals and sign-offs

Quadrant 4 (Bottom Right): **Not Urgent & Not Important MINIMIZE OR ELIMINATE**

Tasks that don't significantly contribute to team goals and should be avoided.

- Excessive email chains without clear decisions
- Unproductive meetings with no clear outcomes
- Low-impact "nice to have" projects
- Frequent context-switching due to unclear priorities
- Reactive work driven by poor planning

Servant Leaders understand that proper prioritization serves not only the team's need for direction but also protection. This method simplifies the team's workflow and empowers them to communicate better when emerging "fires" threaten their focus. When everyone understands what matters most, it's easier to say "no" to distractions and "yes" to meaningful progress.

The Crap Umbrella: Shielding from Dysfunction

Have you ever encountered a *Seagull Manager?* It's a humorous but painfully accurate term describing a leader who swoops in, squawks loudly, craps all over everything and then flies away. Maybe you've experienced it firsthand—something goes wrong, and a rarely-seen senior leader suddenly appears, voices their displeasure, panics a little, and issues a series of unreasonable demands. Then, just as quickly, they disappear, leaving you and your team to clean up the mess.

A Servant Leader, however, does something different. They hold up the "crap umbrella"—shielding their team from unnecessary stress, distractions, and dysfunction. But what does that actually look like in practice?

Raising the Umbrella Against Workplace Seagulls

Seagulls don't just show up when things go wrong. They take many forms—political seagulls, toxicity seagulls, dysfunction seagulls, and overwork seagulls. No organization is immune to these birds circling above, waiting for the perfect moment to disrupt progress. While your team is focused on executing key priorities, their heads are down, unaware of the chaos brewing until it's too late. That's why *your* role as a Servant Leader is to be the watchful eye in the sky—to spot trouble early and step in before it derails your team.

Mistakes are inevitable when teams push their limits. When the "blame game" seagull arrives, Servant Leaders don't point fingers; they take responsibility. If a team member makes a mistake, chances are you played a role in it as their leader—maybe by failing to set clear expectations, providing insufficient feedback, or not offering the proper support. A Servant Leader understands that one of the unfortunate rules of leadership is that *everything is your fault*—because leadership means being accountable for everything the team does or fails to do.

Shielding the team from blame doesn't just inspire loyalty and build trust—it creates a culture where people feel safe to take risks, innovate, and stretch themselves. When employees know their leader has their back, they're far more likely to step up and take ownership. In contrast, when they fear retribution, they retreat into playing it safe, doing only what's required. A Servant Leader allows "failing forward" mistakes that aid in personal and professional growth. They help reframe failure as a learning opportunity, not a career death sentence.

Filtering Out Politics and Dysfunction

Beyond protecting against blame, Servant Leaders also shield their teams from the unnecessary stress of office politics and organizational dysfunction. They do this not by pretending issues don't exist but by filtering out distractions and focusing the team on what *truly* matters.

For example, I once coached a CEO caught in the middle of a heated policy dispute between his subsidiary and the parent organization. On the surface, it was a debate about systems and processes. But underneath? It was a power struggle—a toxic mix of politics, competing egos, and hidden agendas.

This CEO was highly self-aware and realized his frustration was unintentionally seeping into his team. He did his best to share only what was relevant without venting about the politics surrounding the decisions, but sometimes, his emotions got the best of him. During a session, we discussed how his venting—though understandable—was causing anxiety among his people, making them feel powerless against forces outside their control. He committed to a shift: rather than sharing every internal struggle, he focused on what they could control. By reinforcing stability, maintaining transparency without oversharing, and coaching his managers to navigate change with confidence, he was able to keep his team engaged and productive. Over time, not only did his engineers feel more secure, but his reputation as a steady, solutions-oriented leader earned him greater influence in the company—allowing him to advocate for long-term structural changes that reduced the dysfunction at its source.

Another of my coaching clients, a VP of Engineering at a mid-sized tech firm, struggled to shield his team from organizational dysfunction. His company had recently undergone a leadership shake-up, and tensions were high between different business units. Competing priorities, conflicting directives, and backdoor decision-making created chaos, and his engineers—who thrived on clarity and focus—were growing frustrated. Instead of letting his team get caught up in the dysfunction, we developed a strategy to filter out the noise. He set up clear boundaries, ensuring his team only focused on priorities that aligned with company objectives, and he took on the role of buffer—handling political battles himself rather than letting them trickle down.

Protecting Against Overwork and Burnout

Another crucial role of a Servant Leader is protecting their team from overwork and burnout—a growing challenge in today's always-on culture. With endless demands and limited resources, it's easy for teams to run themselves into the ground. This is where a leader must model balancing work ethic with self-care. Work-life balance isn't a static state—it's a rhythm of high-intensity sprints followed by intentional recovery periods. Teams that never slow down eventually break down. Servant Leaders ensure their people recover between major pushes, preventing burnout before it happens.

But here's the problem: Even when time off is available, people hesitate to take it. Vacation anxiety is real. Employees stress about leaving unfinished work, dread the flood of emails waiting when they return, and fear being perceived as "not a team player." So what do they do? They take their laptops on vacation, checking emails poolside, never truly disconnecting.

Servant Leaders can break this cycle by redistributing key tasks while people are out so they feel covered and can truly unplug. They must also set clear expectations for communication while on vacation and reinforce that rest is essential. Finally, they must be an example and normalize time off by taking PTO themselves. Servant Leaders encourage people to unplug guilt-free—because a rested, refreshed employee is far more valuable than one running on fumes.

Protecting the Culture

While a leader has many roles and responsibilities, none is more critical than managing and protecting their team's culture. My favorite definition of culture is *"the way we do things around here."* A team's culture consists of its values, behaviors, symbols, and shared assumptions. It may not always be formally documented, but everyone operates under a set of unspoken rules. The challenge is that culture, being largely unconscious, is easily influenced. An unhealthy culture can take root if a leader allows dysfunction to fester. That's why actively managing team culture is a non-negotiable leadership responsibility.

The Leader's Shadow

Managing team culture starts with managing yourself. There's a saying: *"The shadow of a leader."* This refers to the lasting impact a leader has on their team's behavior through their actions, words, priorities, and what they choose to measure. In other words, leaders shape culture not only through what they personally do and say but also through what they encourage and tolerate from others.

> **"The culture of an organization is shaped by the worst behavior a leader is willing to tolerate."**
>
> *- Steve Gruenert & Todd Whitaker*
> *authors of "School Culture Rewired"*

Perhaps you've seen this firsthand. A highly competitive leader who rewards only top performers creates a culture where employees constantly feel pressured to prove their worth. This might be beneficial in a results-driven environment, but it can backfire in a setting that requires collaboration. The key takeaway? All leaders cast shadows. Servant Leaders intentionally ensure their shadows foster the right behaviors that will produce desired results.

Making the Invisible Visible

The first step in managing a team's culture is to "make the invisible visible" by putting language around the team's operating norms. One powerful method is creating a *Team Manifesto*, a social contract that outlines shared values, assumptions, and expectations. Ask your team:

- How do we want to work together?
- What defines a good teammate?
- What behaviors are unacceptable on this team?
- What are our preferred communication styles and routines?
- How do we handle mistakes and resolve conflict?
- What are our formal (and informal) roles and responsibilities?

Facilitate a healthy dialogue and document their answers. Not only does this exercise foster alignment, but it also gives the leader clarity on what they need to model and reinforce.

Holding the Line on Standards

Many leaders prefer to avoid conflict, making the idea of "enforcing" team culture uncomfortable. However, maintaining team standards is a crucial aspect of leadership. Consider this scenario:

You're leading a brainstorming session, and your team values deep listening and mutual respect. Yet, as Tina presents an idea, Jim repeatedly interrupts her. You hesitate—Jim might get embarrassed if you call him out. But what happens if you *don't* intervene?

A leader is always on stage, and you can bet that if you're uncomfortable, so is everyone else. If you let it slide, the cultural standard shifts—interrupting becomes acceptable. However, if you step in and say, "Let's allow Tina to finish," you reinforce the team's values.

Enforcing culture isn't about controlling people—it's about serving them. Even Jim benefits. He may not even realize he's interrupting, and without your intervention, his credibility among peers might suffer. A Servant Leader holds the line, ensuring that the team's culture remains intact and that individuals have the guidance they need to grow.

Remember, *"If not you, then who?"* Who will uphold the team's standards if you don't? Leadership isn't just about setting expectations—it's about consistently reinforcing them. Formal authority plays a crucial role in shaping team dynamics. People naturally look to their leader to define what is acceptable and what is not. If you're leading a team, understand that all eyes are on you. Your actions—or inactions—send a message.

Psychological Safety: The Culture Amplifier

A thriving culture is one where psychological safety exists. If you're unfamiliar with the term, it may sound like a complicated way of saying *trust*, and while the two are related, they're not identical. Trust is about individual relationships, whereas psychological safety is about team dynamics.

For example, I may trust *you* personally and feel comfortable sharing an opinion in private. But in a team meeting, I may withhold that same opinion for fear of being judged. Perhaps I'm lower in the hierarchy and assume my input isn't valued. If we lack a collective expectation that all voices matter, I won't risk speaking up because we lack psychological safety.

Psychological safety became a buzzword in the mid-2010s when Google released findings from *Project Aristotle*, its internal research on what makes teams effective. After two years of rigorous analysis—including over 200 interviews and data from 180 teams—Google's People Analytics team identified five key factors, ranking psychological safety as the most critical. The highest-performing teams scored significantly higher in this area than less effective teams.

I had the privilege of training hundreds of managers at Google during this period, and psychological safety quickly became the cornerstone of the company's team development initiatives. It was such a game-changer that we immediately integrated it into our Flagship New Manager Training Program, and it became the most significant focus for enhancing team performance.

Assessing Psychological Safety in Your Team

How do you know if psychological safety exists within your team? Ask yourself:

- Do team members constructively challenge one another?
- Do they genuinely have each other's best interests at heart?
- Do they listen empathetically without judgment?
- Can they be vulnerable, openly sharing mistakes and challenges?

Alternatively, you can evaluate psychological safety by looking for behaviors that degrade it:

- Do the real conversations happen in backchannels instead of meetings?
- Are mistakes held against people rather than used as learning opportunities?
- Do team members undermine one another?
- Are people excluded or dismissed for thinking differently?

If your gut tells you that any of these issues are present—even on a minor level—someone on your team likely feels unsafe. That's normal. Every team goes through ups and downs in psychological safety. What matters most is recognizing the signs and taking intentional steps to foster a culture of openness and trust.

Serving the Need for Protection

Many leaders easily overlook the responsibility of protecting the team. They dismiss distractions and organizational dysfunction as unavoidable or simply part of "playing the game." But Servant Leaders see it differently. They understand that shielding their team isn't just about maintaining productivity—it's a powerful act of care that fosters trust and loyalty.

A Servant Leader prioritizes high-value work, ensuring the team stays focused and gains momentum. They act as a buffer against organizational toxicity, preventing unnecessary stress and distractions from derailing progress. Finally, they actively shape the team's culture, reinforcing behaviors that foster psychological safety and collaboration.

When leaders protect their teams well, they earn results in the present and loyalty that lasts into the future. A team that feels safe, valued, and empowered will go above and beyond—not just because they have to, but because they want to.

Self-Assess

How well do you protect your team's focus from distractions?

1-----------2------------3------------4------------5------------6------------7

We are always firefighting because everything feels urgent & important

The real priorities receive the majority of our time and attention

How well do you protect your team from the "seagulls?"

1-----------2------------3------------4------------5------------6------------7

Dysfunction, politics, and burnout are unavoidable

I relentlessly shield my team from these toxic influences

How deliberately do you manage the culture of your team?

1-----------2------------3------------4------------5------------6------------7

Team culture is something that naturally manifests on its own

I communicate cultural expectations and actively enforce those standards

How much psychological safety exists on your team?

1-----------2------------3------------4------------5------------6------------7

Some people are not able to fully speak their minds

People trust they can bring up ideas, questions, concerns, or mistakes.

Scoring:

24-28 = Congrats! Your team likely feels safe and protected

13-23 = Your team likely feels somewhat protected but likely needs more cover to operate at their highest levels of performance

4-12 = Protection may be an underserved need on your team

Reflect

What quadrant of the Eisenhower Matrix needs the most attention right now? What tasks are currently wrongly prioritized?

Which potential seagulls (toxicity, politics, blame game, ridiculous requests, overwork, etc.) are most likely to appear in your organization? What actions can you take to provide the right cover and limit impact?

How has your leadership shadow impacted your team's culture? How have your personality and style shaped your team's behavior?

Recap

- Our primal need for safety still drives workplace behavior. Just as ancient tribes looked to leaders for physical protection, today's teams look to their leaders to shield them from stress, chaos, and dysfunction.
- Modern "threats" are psychological and organizational. These include unrealistic demands, political drama, shifting priorities, and burnout.
- Servant Leaders protect focus. They guard their team's time and energy from distractions, shield against "fire drills," and advocate for priorities.
- Prioritization is protection. Use tools like the Eisenhower Matrix to help your team clarify priorities and stay aligned.
- The "crap umbrella" is real. Great leaders shield their teams from blame, politics, and unproductive noise so they can stay engaged and effective.
- Rest is strategic. Model and protect recovery time to prevent burnout and sustain long-term performance.
- Culture is a leader's shadow. What you say, do, tolerate, and reward shapes how your team operates. Servant Leaders consciously shape a healthy, resilient culture.

13

THE NEED FOR CONNECTION

Humans are inherently social and cooperative creatures. Without this instinct, we likely wouldn't have survived. Unlike other species, we don't have fangs, claws, shells, or venom to defend ourselves. Instead, we have highly developed brains that allow us to create tools and, more importantly, plan and organize together. We may be vulnerable individually, but collectively, we are the dominant species on Earth. This is why being banished from the tribe in a hunter-gatherer society was effectively a death sentence—and why solitary confinement remains one of the harshest punishments in modern prisons. No matter how strong, intelligent, or independent we are, at some point, we all need the support of others. Over thousands of years, we've evolved skills that enhance collaboration and teamwork—because our survival has always depended on it.

We've also become exceptionally attuned to how we relate to various groups. We constantly ask ourselves, "*Do I belong here? Are these my people? Can I trust them? Will they have my back when things get tough?*" We align with groups that reinforce our identity, values, and sense of belonging. Take my friend John, for instance. He's not just an individual; he's White, male, American, Republican, Protestant, Texan, and a die-hard Dallas Cowboys fan. While not everyone who shares these demographics will be John's best friend, he will naturally feel a stronger connection to those with similar identities. Now, imagine John traveling to India for work, and his client invites him to a cricket match. Surrounded by a crowd of Hindi-speaking fans cheering for a sport he doesn't understand, he might feel isolated and disconnected from the environment and the people around him. Our modern tribes—whether cultural, political, or recreational—shape our identity, validate our beliefs, and give us purpose.

Take a moment to reflect on the tribes you consider yourself a part of. How committed are you to those identities? If you're like most people, your loyalty and commitment run deep. For instance, I felt such a strong bond with American values that I risked my life to protect them while serving in the U.S. Army. Turn on CNN or Fox News, and you'll see pundits fiercely advocating for their political party's identity. Watch the Olympics, and it's hard not to feel a surge of pride for your country's athletes. We cheer passionately for our tribes because their success feels like our own. Tribal identity isn't just about affiliation—it's about belonging. It energizes us, fuels our motivation, and drives our loyalty.

Now, imagine if that same level of commitment existed in your workplace team. What if your people truly identified with being part of something greater? The good news is—they want this. Everyone craves belonging. The result is the same whether that sense of connection comes from a sports team or a company culture. People want to feel that their work matters, that they are part of something meaningful. Yet, in many workplaces today, employees feel like members of a work group rather than a real team. They clock in, focus on individual tasks, and rarely see how their contributions impact the bigger picture. Many leaders either don't know how to build high-performing teams or don't invest the time necessary to foster deep connections.

That's a costly mistake. Strongly connected teams don't just perform better—they *thrive.* They communicate more effectively, innovate more frequently, and demonstrate greater resilience. They are more engaged, work harder, and are far less likely to leave. A Servant Leader refuses to let that potential go untapped. They prioritize fostering genuine camaraderie, creating a shared purpose, and turning a disconnected workgroup into a high-performing tribe.

Fostering Connection

Let's start by defining what it means to be *connected* as a team. It's not about being perfectly in sync or becoming best friends with your coworkers (in case you were worried). Workplace connection can mean different things to different people, but at its core, it starts with relating to one another on a deeper level. When I understand who you are as a person—your background, values, and thought process—I naturally feel more connected to you. The challenge is: How can a leader foster this kind of personal exchange in a professional setting?

Let's face it—most employees come to work "buttoned up." Revealing who they genuinely are feels risky. What if my coworkers don't like the real me? What if my values don't align with theirs? To avoid potential judgment, people put on professional facades and stick to surface-level interactions. This often results in shallow, inauthentic workplace relationships.

Tuckman's Stages of Team Development

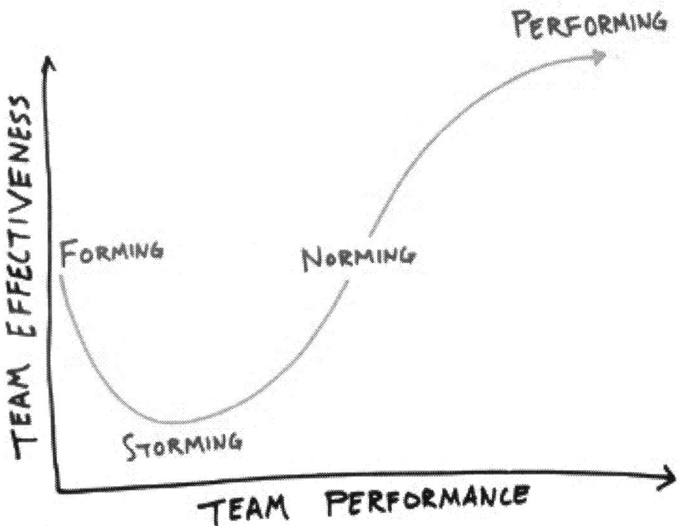

This is particularly true when teams are still in the *Forming* stage of Tuckman's Stages of Team Development Model (1965). People are on their best behavior at this stage, carefully assessing boundaries, expectations, and unspoken rules. Unfortunately, many teams never progress beyond this phase because of fear, anxiety, or ineffective leadership. Moving into the *Storming* phase—where real, constructive conflict occurs—requires vulnerability. Only when individuals feel safe enough to express themselves honestly can trust begin to form. Through trust, real connection emerges, and teams can transition to the *Norming* and *Performing* stages of development.

So, as a leader, how can you encourage this kind of openness within your team? The truth is, you *can't* force authentic conversations—but you *can* create the conditions where they occur naturally. And that starts with getting people together more often. If the idea of spending time with your coworkers makes you cringe, hear me out.

The Impact of Remote Work on Connection

COVID-19 drastically disrupted our workplaces, and many teams never fully recovered. While remote work made connecting more efficient, we traded quality for convenience, and the depth of workplace relationships suffered. Unsurprisingly, weaker relationships led to inferior results, particularly in industries where creativity and innovation depend on trust. [22]

To combat this, many companies have implemented return-to-office mandates or hybrid models to encourage collaboration. While some embrace the chance to reconnect with their office colleagues, others miss the flexibility of remote work. Leaders today face the challenge of finding the right balance between promoting connection and respecting personal time.

Three Ways to Foster Connection

If you want your team to bond more deeply, start with these three simple but effective strategies:

1. **Interact Frequently in Short Bursts.**
   You don't need multi-day offsites to build strong relationships. What works better is consistent interactions in small doses. At a minimum, schedule two 30-minute team meetings per week or a single one-hour meeting. Some teams thrive on short daily stand-ups—15-minute huddles

where everyone stands (versus sits) to promote efficiency. The goal is to create frequent, structured opportunities for team members to engage.

2. **Get People Out of Their Bubble.**
   Office environments can make people feel constrained, discouraging them from showing vulnerability. Change the setting. Host a team lunch, grab coffee together, or plan a casual happy hour. And here's the key: Make it a "no talking shop" zone. The goal is for people to connect as humans, not rehash work topics.

3. **Carve Out Time for Social Conversations.**
   Dedicate the first 5–10 minutes of team meetings to something fun and personal. Ask questions like:
   - What's on your bucket list?
   - What's the first concert you ever attended?
   - What's a food that reminds you of your childhood?

These lighthearted conversations uncover shared interests, allowing team members to relate on a more personal level. If you need ideas, a quick internet search for "conversation starters" will give you plenty to work with.

Creating a Shared Identity

Building deeper relationships is only part of the equation. To create a truly connected team, you must establish a shared identity—a collective sense of purpose and belonging. This is "who the team members want to be and what they want to achieve."[23] A strong team identity transforms a group of talented individuals into a cohesive unit. It provides a common purpose that transcends personal differences. While diverse teams often experience more initial friction, research consistently shows that they outperform homogenous ones.[24]

One of the best examples of shared identity comes from the U.S. Army. When you join a unit, you quickly notice how different everyone is. The Army recruits people from every race, religion, socioeconomic background, and region in the country. A typical platoon resembles a United Nations meeting more than a homogenous group. Yet, despite their vast differences, soldiers operate as a single, unified team. How? Through shared identity.

Every soldier, regardless of background, adopts the belief that they are part of something greater than themselves. The saying "we all bleed green" reinforces that their bond transcends race, religion, and politics. Beyond the Army as a whole, soldiers also develop a fierce loyalty to their Brigade, Battalion, Company, and Platoon. With each smaller unit, identity becomes more distinct, and pride deepens.

Applying Team Identity in Business

Cultivating a shared team identity in a corporate setting may be difficult, but it *is* possible. Here's how to start:

1. **Define Your Team's Purpose.**
    - Don't just repeat your company's mission statement.
    - Ask: Who benefits from the work we do?
    - Have the team write a one-sentence statement that captures what they deliver and who they serve. Here's an example format.

Our Team ____________________ to ____________________

What our team does/delivers — Our most important stakeholder(s)

so that ____

Our intended impact and outcomes

Adapted from Gustavo Razzetti's Team Purpose Canvas (www.fearless culture.com)

2. **Establish a Team Manifesto.**
    - Define how the team will work together.
    - Clarify shared values, expectations, and operating principles.
    - Use this as a guide for decision-making and resolving conflicts.
3. **Set Meaningful, Collective Goals.**
    - Review the SMART goal-setting framework (covered in Chapter 9 – *The Need to Be Challenged*).
    - Involve the team in setting objectives to ensure maximum buy-in.

- Align team goals with individual motivations and strengths.

Fostering connection and building a shared identity takes deliberate effort, which is why highly connected teams are rare. Yet, Servant Leaders know the payoff is immense. Connected teams are healthier, more enjoyable to work on, and produce superior results. Create the conditions for your team to connect, and watch them soar to new heights.

Building Camaraderie

Think of the best team you've ever been part of. What made it stand out from the rest? You're probably recalling trust, authenticity, mutual support, and shared effort. But more importantly, how did it *feel* to be on that team? Maybe you felt respected, valued, energized, proud—even loved. And what was the team's energy like? It was likely playful, creative, and full of momentum. Sure, you worked hard, but it probably didn't feel like a grind. That's because teams with strong camaraderie want to work hard for each other. They enjoy spending time together. They respect each other enough to poke fun at each other, share laughs, and push through tough times side by side.

You know exactly what I mean if you've ever been part of a team with that kind of bond. Even if you hadn't seen each other in years, you could reconnect with those teammates in minutes—picking up right where you left off.

Reflecting on the best teams I've been part of, I still feel a deep connection to those fantastic people and what we accomplished together. I think of my 1993 Fairfax High School basketball team, a scrappy squad that finished the season 22-3. We all knew our roles, worked incredibly hard, and believed in each other. We lacked size but made up for it with an unshakable winning mentality and relentless teamwork. The camaraderie was off the charts. The jokes were endless, and the locker room and bus rides after games were always filled with laughter. What a team that was!

I also think of my time with 1-1 Cavalry in Germany. My Apache Troop brothers were some of the best people I've ever known. Our camaraderie carried us through many grueling challenges. While we were professional and serious during missions, we always found ways to keep things light. I remember many freezing cold nights in Grafenwöhr watching our Cavalrymen during Tank/Bradley qualification tables. Sleep-deprived and fueled by endless cups of coffee, we accomplished our mission and had fun doing it.

None of this was accidental. On both teams, we deliberately worked to build camaraderie. We spent time together, both at work and during personal hours. We organized events, shared experiences, and created stories, rituals, and traditions unique to our team. Over time, these efforts forged unbreakable bonds. The same can happen for your team if you commit to proven team-building processes. Servant Leaders understand the importance of building camaraderie and focus on three key areas: **planning team-building activities, creating crucible moments,** and **celebrating successes**.

1. **Planning Team-Building Activities**

   Oh no! Not the dreaded team-building activities. I hope I didn't just trigger Trust Fall PTSD! Yes, team-building sometimes gets a bad rap for being forced or cheesy. But when done right, it can have a powerful impact.

   Instead of grand, time-consuming events, focus on consistent, bite-sized interactions that build relationships naturally.

   - **Short and frequent:** Once a month, incorporate light games like *Trivia Contests, Two Truths and a Lie, Taboo,* or *Charades*. These quick, engaging activities help teams unwind and bond.
   - **Quarterly outings:** Plan slightly bigger activities like an *Escape Room, Scavenger Hunt,* or *Bowling Night.*
   - **Annual traditions:** Each year, host a major team event, such as a holiday party, an offsite retreat, or a community service day.

   If budget is a concern, plan early. Don't wait until you realize, "Wow, we haven't done anything together in months!" Be proactive—advocate for your budget, show leadership how team-building contributes to business outcomes, and prioritize it.

2. **Creating Crucible Moments**

   Nothing strengthens a team like adversity. While challenging situations are often unpleasant, they're invaluable for building camaraderie. Crucible moments—major obstacles with real consequences—force teams to rely on each other. The term "crucible" comes from the container medieval alchemists used to transform base metals into gold. Similarly, crucible moments can transform your team into a cohesive, high-performing unit. To create crucible moments for your team:

- **Set at least one BHAG (Big Hairy Audacious Goal) each year.** Make it bold enough that people initially shake their heads in disbelief. Inspire them to rally together and rise to the challenge.
- **Lean into adversity.** Crucible moments can be planned or emerge organically. For example, if a competitor launches a disruptive innovation, don't panic—turn it into a crucible moment. Challenge your team to outthink and outmaneuver them. When your company undergoes a major change, frame it as an opportunity to lead the charge.
- **Increase the difficulty over time.** Your team must have a strong foundation before tackling transformational challenges. Build camaraderie first, then apply progressively greater challenges.

In the Army, we had a few humorous phrases for this phenomenon—"Embrace the Suck" and "Trauma Bonding." We often operated in miserable conditions, but instead of resisting, we learned to lean in and find humor in the struggle. Those shared hardships forged lifelong bonds.

3. **Celebrating Successes**

   Too often, leaders overlook the power of celebrating wins. They get so focused on execution and the next task that they forget to acknowledge achievements. This is a missed opportunity. Failing to recognize hard work and sacrifice is demoralizing. Yet, it happens all the time—a quick "thank you" or individual recognition, then back to the grind. Don't make this mistake. Here's how to celebrate success effectively:

   - **Create frequent wins.** If your team is tackling a big challenge, break it into smaller milestones. Each achievement should feel like progress, not just a step toward an impossible end goal. Seek to celebrate progress weekly.

- **Match the celebration to the win.** Small wins might warrant a heartfelt email. Medium wins could call for cake and beer. Big wins deserve a celebratory meal or awards ceremony.
- **Emphasize the journey.** If you want camaraderie to thrive, you must celebrate the journey—not just the destination. Acknowledge the challenges your team overcame, the obstacles they pushed through, and the resilience they demonstrated. Wins fuel momentum, but pride in the shared struggle strengthens bonds, creating a team that stands together through future challenges.

The Legacy of Connection

Attending to the *Need for Connection* is one of the most critical responsibilities of a Servant Leader. Without it, teams stagnate or fail to reach their potential. Deliberately create spaces for team members to connect authentically and build a shared identity. Foster camaraderie through planned activities, crucible moments, and celebrations. When you do, your team won't just perform better—they'll create memories and bonds that last a lifetime. Be the leader who builds a team people talk about for years to come.

Self-Assess

How much does your team enjoy each other's company?

1-----------2------------3------------4------------5------------6------------7

We only talk about our work and relationships are superficial

We deliberately carve out social interaction time and enjoy each other

How strong is your team's shared identity?

1-----------2------------3------------4------------5------------6------------7

We've never talked about what our shared identity is

We know who we are and what we want to achieve together

How likely is it that your team will face a crucible moment?

1-----------2------------3------------4------------5------------6------------7

Probably not this year; we are mostly on cruise control

We have a BHAG in front of us that will require us to bond together

How often do you collectively celebrate team successes together?

1-----------2------------3------------4------------5------------6------------7

We recognize individual contributions but rarely team wins

We seize every opportunity for a team party we can

Scoring:

24-28 = Congrats! Your team likely feels strongly connected to each other

13-23 = Your team likely feels moderately connected with one another but might benefit from greater camaraderie

4-12 = Connection may be an underserved need on your team

Reflect

When was the last time your team participated in a team-building activity? What simple, low-effort activity could you plan that might significantly impact team cohesion?

What stage of team development would you place your team at?

a. Forming - we have new team members and/or act politely.
b. Storming - team members often engage in conflict.
c. Norming - we've settled our differences and established expectations for working together.
d. Performing - we are firing on all cylinders and know how to collaborate effectively.

What steps can your team take to progress to the next stage—or sustain high performance if you're already there?

Recap

- Tribal identity drives loyalty. We align with groups that reflect our values and beliefs, which fosters a deep sense of belonging.
- Disconnected teams underperform. Without a shared sense of purpose, employees feel isolated and disengaged.
- Servant Leaders create safe, consistent opportunities for team members to relate, trust, and open up—both personally and professionally.
- Start with frequent, low-pressure interactions. Short, regular meetings, social time, and casual conversations foster authentic connection and psychological safety.
- Establish a shared identity. Define team purpose, values, and goals together to align everyone around a common mission.
- Camaraderie supercharges culture. Through shared experiences, team rituals, and overcoming challenges together, bonds deepen. Servant Leaders plan team-building, create crucible moments, and celebrate success to reinforce unity

CALL TO ACTION

"The best way to find yourself is to lose yourself in the service of others."

— Mahatma Gandhi

14

SERVANT LEADERS WANTED

If you've made it this far into the book, you're likely committed to being a Servant Leader. That's admirable—mainly because you understand what that truly means. It's a life of sacrifice, hard work, dedication, and commitment. It's the selfless choice to put the needs of others before your own. It also requires reevaluating your definition of success. No longer is success about personal accomplishments. Servant Leaders measure success by their impact on others.

And let's be honest—there are no immediate perks for choosing this path. The rewards of service often reveal themselves much later, sometimes when you least expect them. Yet, you choose to serve anyway. Why? Because deep down, you realize being a Servant Leader isn't just a choice—it's your calling. It's not that you've decided to serve; it's that you've been *chosen* to serve. You serve because you know it's who you're meant to be, and the impact you'll leave on others is worth every challenge along the way.

> **"Everybody can be great because anybody can serve."**
>
> *- Dr. Martin Luther King Jr.*

Maybe you're already in a leadership position and want to apply more of a Servant Leader's approach. Or perhaps you're an aspiring leader who hasn't yet led a team. The good news is that no matter where you are on your leadership journey, Servant Leadership is available to you. It doesn't require exceptional talent, a fancy title, or years of experience. It requires no formal education, promotion, or certification. Why? Because leadership is an activity—one that anyone can choose to perform. Anyone can choose to be more attuned to others' needs and serve them. The moment you make that choice, you become a Servant Leader.

If you're in a formal leadership role, I urge you—don't delay in adopting Servant Leadership. Your people need your leadership now! Over the last 15 years, I've interacted with and observed thousands of managers and noticed a glaring gap—Servant Leadership is often missing in organizations. Yes, I've encountered exceptional outliers—leaders who embodied the principles of service. But they are not the norm. That's precisely why I wrote this book.

From my perspective, Servant Leadership is the only way to lead today, especially given the younger generation's reluctance to follow traditional command-and-control leadership styles. Today's workforce thrives under empowering, values-based leadership. So, why don't we see more of it?

Is it because leaders "don't know what they don't know" and haven't been exposed to the concept? Could it be that many find resources on Servant Leadership too theoretical and struggle with practical application? Or is it simply too hard for leaders to override their innate self-interest and choose to serve? After reflecting on these possibilities, I realized something: Servant Leadership is best learned by working for Servant Leaders and experiencing their impact firsthand. That's how I came to appreciate it. But if only a handful of leaders in your organization practice it, you might not have that opportunity.

This is why your choice to be a Servant Leader matters so much. By following the guidance in this book, you'll positively impact others' lives. They'll see how you cared for them and enabled their success. You'll earn their respect and admiration, leaving a lasting impression. Some of those you lead will go on to lead others, and they'll likely choose Servant Leadership too. After all, why wouldn't they? It's incredibly gratifying to pass along this gift. If more people embrace Servant Leadership today, its impact will snowball, creating exponentially more Servant Leaders in the future.

The world needs this. Imagine if Servant Leadership became the default approach in every organization. Productivity and engagement would soar.

Employees would go home proud of their work and teams, feeling more present and available for their families and communities. It might sound idealistic, but I wholeheartedly believe Servant Leadership can make the world a better place. People like you can make this vision a reality. Every person who chooses Servant Leadership brings us one step closer to a better world. So, if you're ready to serve and make a difference, there's no better time than now.

Next Steps

To become a Servant Leader, start by answering this fundamental question: *Who do I serve?* In a professional setting, this might be your team, colleagues, clients, senior leaders, or key partners. Identify all the stakeholders who could benefit from your service. Remember, Servant Leadership isn't limited to your professional life. You can also serve your family, spouse, community, or social groups. Life offers countless opportunities to lead through service. Pay attention to where you feel the most energy and passion. Where are you being called to serve? At its core, service is an act of love—not romantic love, but authentic, heartfelt care. Wherever it's easy for you to demonstrate care—that's where you need to serve.

Next, identify where you can have the greatest impact. Who needs your service the most? This depends on your unique abilities and characteristics. Assess where you fit best, understanding that no leader is perfect for every situation. Your passion might draw you to a particular group or effort, but you may not be the right leader for it—and that's okay. It simply means others need your leadership more right now. Winston Churchill was the perfect leader for England during WWII, but his characteristics and style might not have suited less turbulent times. The intersection of your calling, passions, and strengths is where you're best suited to serve.

Once you've identified your ideal fit for service, it's time to take action. Remember, you don't need a formal leadership title to begin. But if you're fortunate enough to lead a team, these principles will immediately apply.

Start by being upfront with your team about how you intend to lead. Too many leaders jump into action without ever discussing their leadership philosophy. Share your commitment to Servant Leadership. Explain that your primary role is to help them succeed and reach their full potential. Let them know you will be attuned to their needs and that open communication will be key. Ask for their feedback, and let them know you'll provide feedback as well. Discuss how they like to receive recognition and how you plan to foster trust and autonomy. Set clear expectations so they understand what kind of leader you will be.

Also, explain how you'll serve the team collectively. Share your intention to co-create a vision with their input. Define the kind of team culture you expect and explain that protecting that culture is one of your biggest responsibilities. Make it clear that you will shield them from unnecessary distractions and toxicity. Highlight the importance of building a shared team identity and having fun together.

If you're already months or years into leading a team, it's not too late to have these conversations. However, your team might need time to adjust if you're transitioning to Servant Leadership. Be transparent about your intentions and why you're adopting this approach.

Cherish the Journey

Leading others is one of life's greatest honors. If you're fortunate enough to have followers, cherish every moment. Leadership opportunities are fleeting, and you never know if another will come your way. Treat each day as a gift, no matter how challenging. Even a bad day as a leader is more rewarding than a good day without the chance to lead. One day, you'll look back on your leadership journey with a smile. Ironically, the toughest moments will often be the ones you remember most fondly. It's the lows that make the highs feel so rewarding.

Remember, leadership is a journey, not a destination. You never "arrive" as a leader because the landscape constantly changes. What worked in the past might not work in the future. Your team, role, organization, or industry will evolve, and you'll need to adapt. Stay open to learning and growing. But no matter what changes, let Servant Leadership remain your foundation. Because while everything else shifts, the principles of Servant Leadership will always be timeless.

Finally, I want to thank you for your service. As a Veteran, I've always appreciated it when people acknowledge my service. But today, I want to acknowledge *yours.* Choosing to be a Servant Leader is not for everyone. It's a path for the worthy few. Your service to others will make a difference in countless lives. Your leadership will make the world a better place. Thank you for allowing this book to be part of your leadership journey. If I can further support you, know I'm always here to serve!

DOWNLOAD YOUR FREE ADDITIONAL RESOURCES

As a thank you for buying this book, I am including a free companion leadership toolkit for you to download. It includes infographics, all the self-assessments, enlarged color versions of the diagrams, and more! Scan the image below with your phone or visit www.davidspungin.com.

If you found this book helpful, I would greatly appreciate a review on Amazon.com. Your recommendation will help spread the word to other potential Servant Leaders, and I'm sincerely grateful for that.

ABOUT THE AUTHOR

David Spungin is a best-selling author, top-rated facilitator, and executive coach for high-performing founders and C-suite leaders.

A graduate of West Point and former U.S. Army Cavalry Officer, David spent nearly a decade leading soldiers—including an extended combat deployment in support of Operation Iraqi Freedom.

After the military, he held leadership roles in both a major construction firm and a federal consulting agency. There, he saw a clear gap: while military leaders inspired through service and purpose, many corporate leaders lacked those same people-focused leadership skills.

Determined to change that, David founded his leadership development firm in 2014. He's since coached or trained over 5,000 leaders at organizations like Google, Lockheed Martin, TIAA, Arrow, Johns Manville, DaVita, and Accenture.

David holds a master's in Organization Development from American University and completed advanced leadership studies at Harvard. Originally from Fairfax, VA, he now lives in Denver, CO.

Follow David on LinkedIn, X, and YouTube for leadership insights. To learn more about his executive coaching and team programs, visit his website.

Website: **davidspungin.com**
LinkedIn: **/in/davidspungin**
YouTube: **@davidspungin**
X: **@davidspungin**

REFERENCES

Ashforth, B.E., and Mael, F. (1989), "Social Identity Theory and the Organization," Academy of Management Review, 14, 20–39.

Autry, J. A. (2001). *The servant leader: How to build a creative team, develop great morale, and improve bottom-line performance.* Prima Publishing.

Bachelder, C. (2015). *Dare to serve: How to drive superior results by serving others.* Berrett-Koehler Publishers.

Bennis, Warren, and Robert J. Thomas. "Crucibles of Leadership." *Harvard Business Review*, 9 Feb. 2002, hbr.org/2002/09/crucibles-of-leadership.

Blanchard, Kenneth H, and Renee Broadwell. *Servant Leadership in Action: How You Can Achieve Great Relationships and Results.* Oakland, Ca, Berrett-Koehler Publishers, Inc., A Bk Business Book, 2018.

Bradberry, Travis, and Jean Greaves. *Emotional Intelligence 2.0.* 2009. San Diego, California, Talentsmart, 2021.

Bungay Stanier, M. (2016). *The coaching habit: Say less, ask more & change the way you lead forever.* Box of Crayons Press.

Campone, Francine, et al. *Innovations in Leadership Coaching: Research and Practice.* Fielding Monograph, 27 Apr. 2020.

Chalmers Brothers. *Language and the Pursuit of Happiness: A New Foundation for Designing Your Life, Your Relationships & Your Results.* Naples, Fl, New Possibilities Press, 2005.

Chapman, Bob, and Rajendra Sisodia. *Everybody Matters: The Extraordinary Power of Caring for Your People like Family*. London, Portfolio Penguin, 2016.

Codreanu, A. (2016). A VUCA Action Framework for A VUCA Environment. Leadership Challenges and Solutions. *Journal of Defense Resources Management, 7*(2), 13th ser.

Collins, Jim. *Leadership Lessons from West Point*. San Francisco, Calif., Jossey-Bass, 2013.

Coyle, Daniel. *The Culture Code*. Random House UK, 2018.

De Pree, M. (1992). *Leadership jazz: The essential elements of a great leader*. Dell Publishing.

Donnithorne, L. (1993). *The West Point way of leadership: From learning principled leadership to practicing it*. Currency/Doubleday.

Expert Panel. "16 Smart Leadership Strategies to Encourage Team Camaraderie." *Forbes*, 29 Sept. 2022, www.forbes.com/councils/forbescoachescouncil/2022/09/29/16-smart-leadership-strategies-to-encourage-team-camaraderie/.

Franklin, Joseph P, and Joe Layden. *Building Leaders the West Point Way: Ten Principles from the Nation's Most Powerful Leadership Lab*. Nashville, Thomas Nelson Publishers, 2007.

Goldsmith, Marshall, and Mark Reiter. *Triggers*. Random House Us, 2016.

Goleman, Daniel, et al. *Primal Leadership: Learning to Lead with Emotional Intelligence*. Boston, Mass., Harvard Business School Press, 2002.

Goleman, Daniel. *Emotional Intelligence*. 1st ed., London, Bloomsbury Publishing, 1995.

Goleman, Daniel. *Focus*. Harper Collins Usa, 2014.

Greenleaf, R. K. (1977). *Servant leadership: A journey into the nature of legitimate power and greatness.* Paulist Press.

Greenleaf, R. K. (1998). *The power of servant leadership.* Berrett-Koehler Publishers.

Haslam, S. A., Reicher, S., Platow, M. & Turner, J. C. (2011). *The New Psychology of Leadership: Identity, Influence, and Power (1st edition).* Amsterdam University Press.

Heifetz, Ronald A, et al. *The Practice of Adaptive Leadership: Tools and Tactics for Changing Your Organization and the World.* Boston, Harvard Business Press, 2009.

Hines, Maribel. "As Humans We Are Biologically Wired with a Need to Connect with Others. We Spend so Much Time "at Work" and Tending to the Multi-Dimensional Aspects of Our Careers That It's in Our Interest to Nurture the Relationships with the People We Work Closely With." *Linkedin.com*, 24 Sept. 2022, www.linkedin.com/pulse/foster-team-connection-make-time-personal-hines-mba-sphr-cplp/.

Hunter, James C. *The Servant: A Simple Story about the True Essence of Leadership.* New York, Crown Business, 2012.

Hollema, T. S. (2018, July 23). *How effective virtual teams create shared identity.* LinkedIn. https://www.linkedin.com/pulse/how-effective-virtual-teams-create-shared-identity-sigillito-hollema/

Katzenbach, Jon R, and Douglas K Smith. *The Wisdom of Teams: Creating the High-Performance Organization.* Boston, Harvard Business Review Press, 1993.

Kerr, James. *Legacy: What the All Blacks Can Teach Us about the Business of Life.* London, Constable, 2013.

Kim Malone Scott. *Radical Candor: How to Get What You Want by Saying What You Mean.* London, Pan Books, 2018.

LeBusque, Mark. *The Little Book of Human.* 11 Mar. 2020.

Lencioni, Patrick. *The Five Dysfunctions of a Team.* San Francisco, Calif., Pfeiffer, 2002.

Lohrenz, C. (2021, December 30). Author Post: "Crucible Moments Are The Keys To Your Success." *Forbes.* https://www.forbes.com/sites/forbesbooksauthors/2021/12/28/crucible-moments-are-the-keys-to-your-success/

Louis David Marquet. *Turn the Ship Around! A True Story of Turning Followers into Leaders.* New York Portfolio Penguin New York Portfolio Penguin, 2015.

Marquet, L. D. (2013). *Turn the ship around!: A true story of turning followers into leaders.* Portfolio.

Maxwell, John C. *Winning with People.* Jaico Publishing House, 2012.

Morgan, Angie, and Courtney Lynch. *Leading from the Front: No-Excuse Leadership Tactics for Women.* New York, N.Y., McGraw-Hill Education, 2006.

Mutizwa, Joe. *Leading without Command.* Partridge Africa, 10 Mar. 2015.

Reuel Khoza. *Attuned Leadership.* Penguin Random House South Africa, 1 Oct. 2012.

Schneider, F. W., Gruman, J. A., & Coutts, L. M. (2012). *Applied Social Psychology: Understanding and Addressing Social and Practical Problems.* Second Edition. Thousand Oaks, CA: Sage

Scott, K. (2017). *Radical candor: Be a kick-ass boss without losing your humanity.* St. Martin's Press.

Sinek, Simon. *Leaders Eat Last: Why Some Teams Pull Together and Others Don't.* New York, Portfolio/Penguin, 2013.

Solansky, S.T. (2011), "Team identification: a determining factor of performance", *Journal of Managerial Psychology*, Vol. 26 No. 3, pp. 247-258.

Stanier, Michael Bungay. *The Coaching Habit: Say Less, Ask More & Change the Way You Lead Forever.* Toronto, On, Canada, Box Of Crayons Press, 2016.

Strock, James M. *Serve to Lead 2.0: 21st Century Leaders Manual.* United States, Serve To Lead Group, 2019.

ENDNOTES

1 The term "servant leader" was first coined by Robert K. Greenleaf in 1970 in the essay "The Servant as Leader." He is considered the founding father of the Servant Leadership movement.

2 Dawkins, R. (1976). *The Selfish Gene.* Oxford University Press.

3 Zenger, J. H., & Folkman, J. (2009). *The extraordinary leader: Turning good managers into great leaders* (2nd ed.). McGraw-Hill.

4 Lieberman, M. (2013, December 27). *Should Leaders Focus on Results, or on People?* Harvard Business Review. https://hbr.org/2013/12/should-leaders-focus-on-results-or-on-people

5 "About West Point | United States Military Academy West Point." *Westpoint.edu,* West Point, 2024, www.westpoint.edu/leadership-center/mcdonald-leadership-conference/about-west-point. Accessed 5 Dec. 2024.

6 Michigan State University. (2016, March 1). Unpredictable bosses more damaging than consistently 'bad' ones, study finds. ScienceDaily. https://www.sciencedaily.com/releases/2016/03/160301131113.htm

7 The "Shopping Cart Theory" Supposedly Determines Who Is a Good Person and Who Isn't." *Https://Scoop.upworthy.com,* 6 Aug. 2023, scoop.upworthy.com/viral-shopping-cart-theory-determines-moral-character-440106-440106-440106.

8 Duckworth, Angela. Grit: *The Power of Passion and Perseverance.* New York ; London ; Toronto ; Sydney ; New Delhi, Scribner, 2016.

9 "Hooah,"is an Army word that began life as the acronym H-U-A for "heard, understood, acknowledged." However, it can mean many things.

In this context, it means we acknowledge that the weather situation is crappy, and we will train anyway because the adversity will us better (but we still don't like it).

10 Rozum, John. "Power Ranking the Greatest Coaching Trees in NFL History." *Bleacher Report,* 2024, bleacherreport.com/articles/1058677-power-ranking-the-greatest-coaching-trees-in-nfl-history. Accessed 5 Dec. 2024.

11 Rock, D. (2008). *SCARF: A brain-based model for collaborating with and influencing others. NeuroLeadership Journal,* (1), 44–52.

12 Lazarus, R. S., & Alfert, E. (1964). The short-circuiting of threat by experimentally altering cognitive appraisal. *Journal of Abnormal and Social Psychology, 69*(2), 195–205. https://doi.org/10.1037/h0044635

13 Pink, Daniel H. *Drive: The Surprising Truth about What Motivates Us.* New York, Ny, Riverhead Books, 2009.

14 Nink, Marco. "Many Employees Don't Know What's Expected of Them at Work." *Gallup.com,* 13 Oct. 2015, news.gallup.com/businessjournal/186164/employees-don-know-expected-work.aspx.

15 Howarth, Josh. "32+ Employee Feedback Statistics (2023)." *Exploding Topics,* 28 Sept. 2023, explodingtopics.com/blog/employee-feedback-stats.

16 Wickham, Natalie. "The Importance of Employee Recognition: Statistics and Research." *Quantum Workplace,* 6 July 2023, www.quantumworkplace.com/future-of-work/importance-of-employee-recognition.

17 Inc, Gallup. "Is Your Industry Delivering on Employee Recognition?" *Gallup.com,* 13 Sept. 2022, www.gallup.com/workplace/400907/industry-delivering-employee-recognition.aspx.

18 Heaphy, E. D., & Losada, M. F. (2004). The role of positivity and connectivity in the performance of business teams: A nonlinear dynamics model. *American Behavioral Scientist,* 47(6), 740–765. https://doi.org/10.1177/0002764203260208

19 Rothaizer, Joel M. "Optimizing Positive Feedback." *Forbes*, 13 Sept. 2023, www.forbes.com/councils/forbescoachescouncil/2023/09/13/optimizing-positive-feedback/.

20 Wikipedia Contributors. “Systems Theory.” *Wikipedia,* Wikimedia Foundation, 25 May 2019, en.wikipedia.org/wiki/Systems_thinking.

21 McKinsey & Company. “Diversity Matters Even More: The Case for Holistic Impact.” *Mckinsey & Company,* 5 Dec. 2023, www.mckinsey.com/featured-insights/diversity-and-inclusion/diversity-matters-even-more-the-case-for-holistic-impact.

22 Clear, J. (2020, June 9). *How to be More Productive by Using the "Eisenhower Box."* James Clear. https://jamesclear.com/eisenhower-box

23 Rummelhart, A. (2017, November 7). *Tuesday tips: The importance of team identity, presented by Spin Ultimate.* Ultiworld. https://ultiworld.com/2017/11/07/tuesday-tips-importance-team-identity-presented-spin-ultimate/

24 Phillips, K. W., Liljenquist, K. A., & Neale, M. A. (2009). *Better decisions through diversity. Kellogg Insight. https://insight.*kellogg.northwestern.edu/article/better_decisions_through_diversity

Made in the USA
Columbia, SC
14 June 2025

d3480323-39ee-4a9e-bb4b-5c901b005501R01